What's wrong with us *Kali* women?

What's wrong with us *Kali* women?

Prose Poems by

Anita Nahal

Cover design by Shay Culligan
Cover art by Anjali Bhardwaj, entrepreneur, graphic artist,
illustrator and animal activist, New Delhi, India

Cover page quote credits:
E. Ethelbert Miller, writer, and literary activist. He is the author
of several collections of poetry and two memoirs. Miller is the host
of the weekly WPFW morning radio show *On the Margin*
Joy Lalita Ford Austin, President and CEO, Joy Ford Austin Arts
and Humanities Advocacy, Washington DC

ISBN: 978-1-954353-88-6

Kelsay Books
502 South 1040 East, A-119
American Fork, Utah, 84003

To my blessing, my son Vikrant, who is my constant companion and support in all my life's journeys, keeping me loved, protected and grounded.

And in the warm memory of my parents,
Drs. Chaman and Sudarshna Nahal,
for wonderous and valuable life lessons.

Acknowledgments

Aaduna, Hey, Spilt Milk Is Spilt, Nothing Else, In All the Spaces—Diverse Voices in Global Women's Poetry Anthology, & Yearbook of Indian Poetry in English: "You are an immigrant too"

AAUW-The Empire State Virtual Branch Newsletter & Hey, Spilt Milk Is Spilt, Nothing Else: "They say people need to unite"

Borderless: "Airplanes: when a heart came to be in crimson and saffron," "Sleepless nights"

Burrow: "Teaching chair yoga at an assisted living home"

But You Don't Look Sick: The Real Life Adventures of Fibro Bitches, Lupus Warriors, and other Super Heroes Battling Invisible Illness Anthology: "I did not say, *I love you,* to my mama"

Confluence & Burrow: "Corona and love-life layers"

Confluence & Hey Spilt Milk is Spilt, Nothing Else: "Blame"

Confluence & In All the Spaces—Diverse Voices in Global Women's Poetry Anthology: "It's not all about sex"

Confluence & Lockdown Prayers Anthology: "Breathe"

Confluence: "Bandit Queen *Phoolan Devi,*" "Jazz vocalist," "Native," "Rape"

FemAsia Zine: "Fallacy of a single, immigrant mom," "What's wrong with us *Kali* women?" "Why I usually cry in the shower"

Hey, Spilt Milk is Spilt, Nothing Else: "Feeling down, being down"

In All the Spaces—Diverse Voices in Global Women's Poetry Anthology: "Smooth operators"

International Journal of Multicultural Literature: "Know your wheel, Homo Sapiens"

Lapis Lazuli International Literary Journal: "Ancient creation," "Blues of a strong Indian woman in mid-America small town"

Mirror of Time: "Uncertainty, my secret lover"

Organizational Aesthetics: "Snoot & snout"

Pandemic Poetry Anthology: "Covid19's inverted triangle"

Paradise on Earth Anthology: "Fire couldn't stop laughing"

Ruptured Anthology: "Diasporic feminism's love making"
Seeking Home Anthology: "Babylon, my sinful dance muse,"
   "Paying my debt in two lands," "Spilt milk in native and
   foreign lands"
*Setu & In All the Spaces—Diverse Voices in Global Women's
   Poetry Anthology:* "Hard: Us, animals, and the aliens," "Chase
   away demons left behind"
*Setu, The Creative Café-Medium, Burrow, & Lockdown Prayers
   Anthology:* "What happened to their clothes?"
Setu: "Democracy in decline," "Gandhi's *chaadar*," "Pity, go take
   a hike," "There's a hole in my heart but my heart is whole"
The Creative Café-Medium: "A woman's age is kicking and alive,"
   "Family blood"
The Dillydoun Review: "Greatest warrior is metamorphotic Mother
   Earth," "My *Trojan* horse" "*Maryada* and modern *Draupadi*"
The Ekphrastic Review: "A new day"
The Kali Project Anthology & Seeking Home Anthology: "Finally,
   she showered"
The Kali Project Anthology: "Homo Sapiens and Hindu Goddesses
   in India and America," "*Kali* asks, 'Two, three, repeated or
   karmic wrongs make a right'?"
The POM-Medium & Poetryspective: "Mom's shoulders"
*The Pom-Medium, Doordarshan Kolkata, Global Poetry Web, &
Organizational Aesthetics Journal: "Covid19 stigma," "Hold on
   baby, we'll soon be home," "The crystal ball is sick and tired,"
   "The Ghost of Covid19" "Snoot or snout"
*The POM-Medium, Pen-in-Hand Literary Journal, &
   Poetryspective:* "How easy it is for a Black life to be taken"
Visual Verse: "Who let the pigs out?"
Writers-Editors-Critics: "Forgotten musical instruments: No words
   for our music," "A Window with a view"

Author's note: The author generally revises her poems, long after
she writes them, and long after these are first published. That's the
only way she believes she can improve on her writings. Therefore,
you might find some of the previously published poems in this
volume have been revised.

Soliloquies, treatises on life and human interactions are the essence of Anita Nahal's prose poems in this eclectic, thought provoking, formidable, haunting, soul reflective collection which is Nahal's third collection of poetry. Inspired by the strength of Hinduism's many female goddesses, especially *Kali*, and by the author journeys across the world, Nahal's poems portray the perceptions of a diaspora Indian woman on immigration, domestic abuse, rape, aging, Covid19, single motherhood, love and sensuality, death, racism, sexism, environment, alien life, environment, poverty, and much more.

Anita says that she generally lives at intersections thereby not limiting herself to one space or manner. As such her poems reflect variously, impressionist, realist, romantic, confessional, and surrealist styles. Looking at life from the prism of tenacity, sensitivity, and survival Nahal's poems display imagery that is starkly varied, vivid and robust. Phyllis Wheatley, Sylvia Plath, Emily Dickinson, and Maya Angelou are some of the writers Anita's poems are compared with. Anita Nahal takes everyday emotions, actions, and reactions, and creates an immensely poignant, unforgettable poetic tapestry.

Contents

What's wrong with us *Kali* women?

There's nothing wrong. Nothing wrong. That's your fear labelling us. We are the *Kali* women. And all other female, male, androgynous gods. We don't distinguish. We seek. We learn. Comprehend. Embrace. We are the *Kali* women. In the forefront, striding and yes, strutting our stuff too. Some men gulp and gawk. Making a tight knot of patriarchy right in front of their balls. They are the same who have been bowing before *Kali*'s statues for centuries. Marking their foreheads with *mitti* from her robes. And then they call her *Ma Kali* and walk away brash, brazen, evil. Don't think she's not watching. There's nothing wrong. Nothing wrong. That's your fear labelling us. We are the *Kali* women. And all other female, male, androgynous gods. Always in front, straddling between pathways, poles, blocks, and behavior. Between screams and footsteps pinning for justice denied. Justice battered. Justice flagged. Murdered. Burned. Their dark skin, their gender, religion, their sandals blood stained, their clothes drenched and smelling of your foul breath, with your hands striking, your feet jutting and hitting. And then some in their sinister voice sing well into the murky night, *Ma Kali. Ma Kali. Ma Kali. Ma Kali.* Don't think she's not watching. There's nothing wrong. Nothing wrong. That's your fear labelling us. We are the *Kali* women. My skin is *kali,* my heart is gold, my soul is a child, cries, laughs, jumps, feelings flow like fresh churned cream from cow's milk. My skin disgusts you. Yet you try to tan yours. My skin disturbs you, yet you find it exotic. My skin you call *gandi.* But I am clean. I bathe. In winters when my skin lightens a bit, you proclaim, I'm looking s*aaf,* fair. I was always clean. It's your mind that is dirty. Even mock bathing in river *Ganga* might skim above your falseness. *Ma Kali. Ma Kali. Ma Kali. Ma Kali.* Don't think she's not watching.

*Mitti: Dirt/Earth *Kali: Of Black color and also Goddess of destroyer of evil *Ma: Mother *Gandi: Dirty *Saaf: Clean, also, a colloquial word to imply fair skinned *Ganga: Considered to be one of the holiest rivers in India

Homo Sapiens and Hindu goddesses in India and America

I left my India one score ago. Arriving at Dulles airport, a sense of excitement laced with trepidation engulfed. Seemed we had boarded a spaceship to another planet never to return. Return was no longer a word I knew, folding it neatly in the white kerchief my father slipped into my hand at the airport between tears and smiles. My mother clasped my fingers, repeating, *"I think you both will not come back to India." "Of course, we will."* I sounded unconvincing. Folks say I am *Durga, Kali, Laxmi,* and *Saraswati,* and all other Hindu goddesses manifest in me. I am grateful yet I don't wish to float on high pedestals. I don't get human hugs often. That touch, that oxytocin making me feel situated with love. And I don't wish for the mean and uncouth Homo Sapiens to pour milk over my statues or feed me heavy sweets while disdainfully shooing beggar children out their way. Or seeking blessings from me—a female—and then raping other females. I also don't want to float my goddesses as exotic to horny Homo Sapiens anywhere in the world. I hid the kerchief in my native memorabilia box taking a whiff every now and then. Fatigued, I drudge along like broken subalterns returning from a long war. Mom and dad have long passed. I became all the goddesses when my son was born. I became all the goddesses when you tried to snatch him from me. I became all the goddesses when you insulted me in public. I became all the goddesses when I rejected you. I became all the goddesses when I decided we must leave. I became all the goddesses when I fended alone for my son. I became all the goddesses when I did not compromise anymore. I became all the goddesses when I did not cry anymore. I became all the goddesses when I signed on the dotted line of the divorce papers in my America.

*Durga: Goddess of war, strength, and protection *Kali: Goddess of the destroyer of evil *Laxmi: Goddess of wealth *Saraswati: Goddess of learning

How easy it is for a Black life to be taken

"I can't breathe, I can't breathe," Eric Garner said. George Floyd said. Who is listening? Who is thinking? Who is cautioning? Justice, injustice. Even roughed edged stones cannot burst tears from those inhuman snatching eyes. Inhuman strangleholds. That flesh in a clinch, that breath in a grip, that blueness, that numbness of death slowly inching. Snapped without a sanity thought. How easy it is for a Black life to be taken. What goes on in the minds of those pinning down innocents? What goes on in the minds of those being pinned down? Or being shot at? Or being pulled over? Or being arrested? Being accosted. Being accused. Being lynched. Burned. Choked. Raped. Extinguished. How easy it is for a Black life to be taken. I can hear their cries. Their sweat bursting on terrified faces. Their running footsteps. Their scarred attire rustling in the fragile wind. I can find no reason. Nor explanations. Rationalizations. Accounts, excuses, none of the details matter as to what's going on in the minds of those pinning down innocents. I don't hear their imagined fear. Their tainted soul. Their body without a heart. Their supercilious, crude beliefs that arrogantly shout, how easy it is for a Black life to be taken. *"I'm just bird watching." "Just talking. Just breathing." "I'm just standing outside the bar." "I'm just jogging down the neighborhood where you stood your entitled ground." "I'm just driving in my own car" "I'm just entering my own home, Not showing any aggressive tone. I did not nettle, ingratiate or fight. Provoke or impregnate. Scuffle or rile."* Why is it so easy a black life to kill? How easy it is for a Black life to be taken. Castile, Floyd, Garner, Blake, Brown, Rice, Bland, Gray, Martin, Arbery, Taylor, Till. Not just any names. They were living. Someone's loved ones. Living. Alive. Stolen. Purloined. How easy it is for a Black life to be taken.

What happened to their clothes?

As I was doing yoga laying on the carpet in my bedroom, I saw my clothes hanging in my open cupboard. They seemed oddly silent. I wondered if I would ever wear any again. To dance? To work? To the grocery store? Or anywhere? Tears swelled up. What happened to the clothes of those who died from Covid19? Are they still hanging in their cupboards? Still waiting to be worn to work, dinner or theatre? Still waiting to wrap their owners' bodies. What happened to their beds and comforters? Are they still waiting to give sleep to their owners? Why am I thinking of inanimate objects, I asked myself? Why wasn't I thinking of their loved ones left behind? I suppose the news of their bodies being quickly driven away by body collectors in hazmat suits, never to be seen by their loved ones again made me cry more for their clothes and bedsheets that their loved ones would never see them in again.

Smooth operators

"What's going on?"
"What is that?"
"Rather queer looking, don't you think?"
"What scrawny legs and arms. Wonder how they can so nimbly move."
"Look at their babies and juveniles, why do they give out that funny squeak?"
"Where are they going? What are they carrying?"
"Be careful not to step on any."
"Just look and observe, see their hands flaying."
"Shh, be quiet, don't want to disturb or scare them away."
"And don't go too near for you never know when they might attack! Watch from a safe distance."

The jungle seemed rather overawed and inaudible. The sloths, the howler monkeys, the white-faced monkeys, spiders, tarantulas, poison dart frogs, armadillos, coatis, agoutis, owls, army ants and ant eaters, and all the birds, a jaguar too, and a caiman, and also an iguana or two sat huddled. Smooth operators. They watched the hordes of humans walking by, tripping, carrying sticks, mumbling incoherently, with torches strapped to their foreheads, cameras and tripods swinging, surging gazes, stopping animatedly to peer through boroughs, holes, and branches high and far between and behind many stratums. Smooth operators. Overhead a spaceship, hidden between dense clouds, its folks peering from each and every window, making sounds like cackling chickens or so my brain has been led to believe by Hollywood's self-absorbing pastime. Smooth operators. Who is watching whom?

19

It's not all about sex

It was pretty dark now and the path was not lit except for the guide's powerful torch which suddenly sprawled on trees tops right in our path. We stood still, whispering, *"What do you see? What do you see?"* Gesturing to follow him, hushing us, fingers turned backwards, and then hands full open in stop. Right above us, a drama was ensuing. The sloths were not frightened by the glaring lights. The new mama with the baby clinging to her breasts was climbing fast. As fast as sloths can when in danger. The stud sloth was in pursuit from another branch. His heat made him faster and he reached right beneath the new mama and then he retracted quite suddenly knowing his heat wasn't going to be satisfied, today. After scratching himself thoroughly, he tried again. The baby sensed something and quite valiantly left his mama to stride up the branch alone. She pulled baby back to her embrace. The stud knew, it was only to be about consideration, today.

Hard: Us, animals, and the aliens

The cage was hard, tight, barely visible to some, in this world, this life, or not. She wasn't sure if she was an animal. If so, which? Or was she an illegal immigrant? A criminal? What did she do? *"Let me out, let me out..."* The air seemed very tight, hard. Where'd the ozone go? The cage seemed artificial. Like a GMO. The cage seemed bogus. Like cosmetic implants. *"Hey, can you see me?"* The cage swung nosily on its hinges, rising with each hard push. The cage was hard, tight. Who was pushing so hard? Exhausted she fell down into tired slumber. The watch was dead. And so was the car battery. *"Hey, do you know the time?"* she asked hard footsteps near the hard cage. Where did I keep my car keys, she scratched her dirty hair? What difference will it make like in Emily Dickinson's *Tis harder knowing its due/Than knowing it is here.* On all fours, she felt the solid, cement floor of the hard cage. Some curious mice, some clueless cockroaches, some ruthless ants seemed to be minding their business. Trying not to walk over her. She seemed too hard. And it was already too hard, too tight in the damp coop crevices of theirs. Some voices could be heard from afar. She didn't know their language *"Hey, hey, who's there?"* Hard silence responded. She pulped it hard and then it swallowed down her inhabitable throat which tightened its hard hold. Scars of many centuries, lifetimes, roam among the particles of creation, of ancient visitors, of planet volcanoes, and formation big bangs. Must be some very hard substances. Where were the hearts and emotions? In a huge pot, brews coagulated plasma. What's underneath, not many want to know. She does. *"I may find my type there. Maybe, beneath the fire they found a hard, tight cave in which to survive?"*. For now, she sits in a room with no lights on, except twinkling ones. The walls are not hard. The people are earnest. Love is abundant. Malefic Saturn might be proceeding out, finally. It's taken many hard beats. The silhouette of her black wrangler jeep outside beckons while droplets of her sweat emitted, sweat petrified, glisten on the windshield. The overhead streetlight shows all. Hard giver. Hard seeker.

Chase away demons left behind

Demons to the right. Demons to the left…. Hey, Tennyson, I gave em the marching orders. The boots are heavy, rains heavier, the load we carry is sometimes, demonic. Teeth barring, jaws clicking. No saluting, just shaming. Frost's woods appear darker, shadier. More dense fog. More muzzle in the thick. More branches splitting at lightest touches, more innuendoes slithering into tiny spaces.
It's packed
Not leaky
No air
Tough to breath. I rise, repeatedly, and the demons pull me down, repeatedly. The trident in my hand did not fall. Neither did my grace. I let the spilt milk run amok. I wasn't gonna be the one wiping it, again and again. The head demon stopped, looked back, gave a nod.
Minor demons
Gathered around
All heads bobbling
Up, down, up, down
I looked away and sat on autonomy, on easy draft, with perfumed flowers, and a glass of red wine. I bade goodnight. No more demons to my right, nor to the left flank they came. Bitterness and anger have gone away, so has the melancholy. I nodded at demons all, gave a toothless smile. And as I turned around, I could hear the gather of dust, the rusted blood, and the bones crumbling one upon another.

Diasporic feminism's love making

I recollect the nervous heartbeats, the terrified footsteps, the hands that broke, the mouth that howled. As patriarchy douses kerosene on many love dreams, the fires that seethe are of odium. As patriarchy stands at the door, unclothed and cruel, escape is livid and stealthy. As patriarchy skins her wetness, it can only scald him, and he'll forever stand rejected. Feminism is not a child of half a seed. Forget love or love making, New Delhi or America, patriarchy and feminism can't be in the same bed. Love making stands behind me in the mirror as I comb my hair, perfuming it with a few oud puffs. It lays its earnest hands on my shoulders, stroking and arousing. *"I know you miss it."* I look up slowly, locking eyes, trying to find the right words. *"Yes... what to do...what to do...very few men have the balls to love with honor. So, I'd be better alone than with a boor."* A resilient, prudent woman doesn't want to be a spiteful boss or bossy in the nights between the sheets and you. Her soul is tired of deceit, not love. Your passion can drive her. Seep in like an innate sip of heated fudge that she can hold between her thighs. Your lips upon hers, your touch caressing her reminds love is the same everywhere. It's only gotta be true. Wait to sink into her slowly. Leave your ego in the laundry basket down the hall. She'll wash and pleat neatly tomorrow and won't even tell you.

A woman's age is kicking and alive

I carry. I carry. I carry my age in a genie's bottle; kicking and alive, finely seared with a recipe from wise women's tales. You must wonder, why I didn't include "old." Excuse me, please, did you not see the NFL half time the other day? With JLo and Shakira strutting their 50's and 40's stuff? I ain't that far ahead. It's a new age, man. Yes, I meant to say, man. That smug macho stuff shoved down formative years and much after. Even when an "old" man may sit beside and ask, with his aging tongue in his crinkling cheek,

"How old are you my dear?"

"Me? What about you?"

"I'm the distinguished one."

"Really, I only see your furrows, crumples, and sags yawning wide all over. And I ain't your dear. Don't you know its rude to ask a woman's age?"

"I thought you were one of the modern ones, mama."

"Yes, and that's why I might kick you stronger in your a...big daddy."

But I carry. I carry. I carry my age in a genie's bottle; kicking and alive, finely seared with a recipe from discerning women's parables. Of coconut oils, Boswellia serrata, cucumber, and fresh un-boiled milk and turmeric potions. Of positivity, tenacity, and spunk. Of refusing to listen to any tell-tale signs. Even those ear-empaling from horrific neon lights. For a woman's age is never known, really. Never told, really. Never asked, really, as she struggles to hide in ways learnt best. Let me take a breather now. Meditate a bit. Just lay down for a while. And sip me some almond champagne. After all, I'm a renaissance woman, a fighter and survivor, a phoenix and Pollyanna, all churning in the tonic of youth that I formulated many decades ago after the sagacious women of my life, with my mother at the helm steered my mind towards the radiating brights in all the lights. Even the piercing ones.

Corona and love-life layers

Layers of love and life are crumbling, some are mixing, some decomposing, some disappearing. Aristotle said humans are social animals, yet some are still unapologetically crude, arrogant, asinine. Some just don't wish to be bothered. Some don't respond or connect. Some are merely self-protecting. Some have no choice over the virus. Some say its punishment. Even animals are ashamed of us. And Gods don't know what more to tell us about kindness and giving. History hasn't been worthy. The slave markets, lynchings, murders, rapes, opulence, greed, gratification, wars, conflicts, boats of begging refugees left to decompose, leaving little kids famished, breathing their last on scalped beaches or with their small bodies burning without recovery, without mothers, crying and dying alone on impersonal makeshift tent hospital beds. Animals were not spared either. There's an unusual hush. So eerie even a skeleton in a cemetery is scared, knocking on tombstones, begging other skeletons to keep him company. Some humans could hear themselves stampeding in grey, opaque skies, densely crowded with cumbersome, soiled clouds standing around menacingly. And the sun didn't want to join the uncalled-for cruel party. Stood afar pondering, *"Shall I give them a bit of geniality? Do they deserve it, yet?"* On the flip, the streets had ample fresh air and the ozone was plumper. Trees too were a lusher green. One strength replaced by the other. Layers had almost collapsed, conflated, almost disappeared, pitch-opaque with cinder still trying to remain alive like enticing smoldering paper edges.

Greatest warrior is metamorphic Mother Earth

Petals adorn my broken self and like our Native ancestors I search for the tale in each. Seeking the shadows of animals that stood with us. Seeking the brothers and sisters that fought with us. The winter fires that sheltered us. Some have roamed the world, seeing, sprouting, waning and passing into dimensions inside us where we go when others treat us different. Don't shake your head and offer pity over my amputated legs. Ask instead, what, where, why they walked, kicked, dragged and slumped upon. How a warrior I was born. Don't nod in understanding without looking straight into my eyes which are still vivacious in my guillotined head on the butcher block. How a warrior I was re born. Don't put your arms around mine without feeling the condensed air that extends beyond my shredded joints. How a warrior I was born, again and again and again. Don't offer to cover me up with your defiled blanket. With your conceited coat. With your carefully sculpted sentences pulling a spoof that you are wise. Don't smirk at distances between loves. Don't try walking on my footprint's ashes still festering. Don't try to clasp my hand to tell a joint story. Don't. Don't. Just watch. Just watch as my remaining petals keep disappearing. Watch the air around you solidify. Watch the ground beneath you reinforce like metamorphic rocks. Watch till I become a whisper at the end of the last drop of water. And then, you can scream.

The above poem was inspired by the work of Australian poet, writer, painter, and sculptor, Elizabeth 'Lish' Škec

Know your wheel, Homo Sapiens

Must know, I must know my wheel. It's pretty sturdy, I think. Of a name, skin, bones, lucks, quirks, genes, memes, heritage, future, parents, prayers for my child, all my voyages, and crossings. My receptacle is a bit older now. Ensuring life as my running mate, I keep greasing my wheel with joy, exercise, food, safety and sex. Maslow would be pleased. I grapple hard though to find a mass of meanings to one profound word, home. Implications stumble aimlessly like round plastic numbers in a lottery wheel. Wheels and circles of plethora identities toss within, sometimes seething, sometimes sobbing, or giggling or mocking self and others. Like Pegasus my hooves dig into the earth, bursting forth fresh springs. Resurgence and I are twins, and the vestiges of my memories don't grow weary. I did not desert my birth wheel. I kept adding, borrowing, chiseling, sometimes imperceptible, discreet, sometimes iridescent and visible. Wonder what picture life's camera conjured of a single mom hungry for peace, holding the hand of a young son in airport line waiting to board the plane. The in-law *Jats* had their wooden canes thumping ferociously, arms flaying, they promised blood revenge. And my clan, the *Punjus,* tittered heartily, seeing only the merriment of departure to gilded cities, not my exertions. None knew the ethos or depth of the storm brewing. If we left, it would be forever. And so, it came to be. Then the western melting pot had me lifted like sincere waves but couldn't always glide back like pro-surfers. Several months it took to pronounce me credential worthy what I'd spent twenty long years in India to establish. Yes, yes, I came by choice, yet ageism and foreign degrees don't make for a palatable drink. And as Covid19 pundits bicker on how, when, where, why and who wrought this plague upon the world, the wheel of countless Homo Sapiens is being renamed, survival.

*Jats: A community in India *Punjus: Short for Punjabis, another community in India *Abraham Maslow: Triangle of hierarchy of needs

A sip of wine

It's not only when I have a sip or two of wine that I miss you. I miss you, always. Not every single moment of each day. But always. Wine only pulls my desires out more wantingly. Nerve endings sink. Feel like falling. Want to let go. Feel your mouth upon mine, again. Love's nemesis is desire. And desire is basic to humans. Love compels some of us to lead mangled lives. Not pretty sights, the missteps, big and small. Trying best to control. A romantic fool, I feel love can be divine. But where are you? In your artificial reality? Hiding? Behind your bloated ego? Are these your potency assets? And my enduring love, a weakness? I seek an illusion of a time long gone. Bound to delusion, I try to unshackle. But when a sip or two of wine waltzes down my throat resting and churning with the juices in my tummy, I miss you more than always. The want, the craving, the kneading, like pliable dough of my sighs. The feathers skim at the stroke. Don't want to change at midnight.

Breathe?

She stood at the banks of the river railings knowing she could breathe. Skyscrapers seemed hold-able. She knew she could breathe. Maybe even pick some up, slide into pockets, and still breathe. It was a bit nippy and city lights seemed welcoming yet far enough not to smother. Most knew they could still breathe. Few joined her for the dawn and dusk spectacular views and these anonymous knew they could still breathe. As she stretched her *Namaste* hands high above her head, her clothes aviating in the taxing wind, she knew she could still breathe. She was a tree, an airplane and a boat, extending and firming. She knew she could still breathe. She saw bias, hate and cruelty, twisting from side to side. She knew some could still breathe. Untimely and unfair deaths screamed from the belly of the water propelling a haunting hymn upwards like a tornado in reverse…

Who can breathe?
Can breathe?
Oh God, tell us, can we breathe?
God, tell us, can we breathe?
Who can breathe?
Can breathe?
Calm our soul, God, tell us, can we breathe?
We don't want not to breathe
Don't want not to breathe
Yes God, we want to breathe
Yes, God, we want to breathe
Protect our souls, God
We want to breathe
Oh God, please, tell us, can we breathe?

*Namaste: Traditional greeting in India

29

Mom's shoulders

As a teen something I used to watch my mom's slim shoulders, seeming young forever. Rounded and glowing. In extreme Delhi heat she'd fan herself with her sari *pallu,* sprinkling water on her skin, and her sleeveless blouse gave me a glimpse of her shoulders. They appeared like those of a young woman. I'm the age now she was then. I watch mine in the mirror. Same as hers. Upon stroking, I find them downy and silky. Maybe now I understand why my mom's shoulders looked so youthful. Continuous yoga, and I presume oils she massaged there, or that she hadn't been truly loved. Shoulders of a young woman.

*Pallu: Corner or side of the sari which falls over the shoulder

Spilt milk in native and foreign lands

It's not easy to define anyone's tip of the iceberg's gory-glory. Tracee Ellis Ross said, *A woman's fury holds lifetimes of wisdom.* They say, most women are more restless than men, a bit more. After all, their heartbeats are preoccupied, a bit more. And if you feel their restlessness leads to anger sometimes, a rebellion sometimes, a certain withdrawal, suspicion, angst, a certain everything kind of trepidation, remember not to merge the silvery moon and the sun's redness. Could be a brawl. Because of you, me and others can be the stories; some fully cooked, some half-baked, though always real. What am I going to do with this, this single mother, woman of color, immigrant story, this? Escaping from abusive memories, aching to create new benign ones. Lots of spilt milk. Rusting and untrusting can be the *almirahs* of our mind. What to hold, hug, or not? Left behind many nightmares. Go now, go; run fast run, take your child and go to a place far away and then some. Can't be the moon or the once declared-non-gratis-poor planet Pluto. It's too far out. Maybe across the oceans. Foreign or home spun, a forced balanced prescription was prayed for, both exultant and upsetting. Most folks want a normalcy may come from their crossings and passages. It is after all, spilt milk. And all that matters in the end is to bathe in and shake hands with the sheen that shines on spilt milk that dries in native or foreign lands.

*Almirahs: Cupboards

Portions of this poem are from onegin stanzas in the author's unpublished novel

31

Paying my debt to two lands

I left my India where as a child I learned to swim in the river *Ganga*. For Hindus, the most sacred waters. My father tied an empty tin box for learners to my chest and guided me into gushing waters in the holy city of *Haridwar*. I was terrified less, mesmerized more by *Ganga* flowing by in all its might signaling at me like a protective grandparent. In the evening, tiny paper boats with lights seemed like fireflies out seeking companionship, and sometimes I saw ashes of cremated Hindus drifting by with only yellow marigolds peeking above the water like solemn pall bearers. Overwhelmed my little frame huddled next to my parents, all of us reflecting in the night waters. It was cultural spirituality attempting to bond with me. I left my India as my ex wouldn't let me be, forcing me to eat my breathing, my emotions, my words, that wanted to express freedom. Now, I live near the Potomac waters of another nation's capital encircling the stately monuments of history in my America. A new bond has been forged. My son will cremate me one day in this land that became our savior keeping only a handful of my ashes to go into the *Ganga,* so that my soul pays its debt to two lands.

*Haridwar: A city in the Indian state of Uttarakhand where the river Ganga or Ganges flows and is considered a holy city for Hindus *Potomac River: Flows between Washington DC and Arlington, Virginia

You are an immigrant too

So, please don't ask where I am from unless your lineage is clear gel, as chained, shackled, sardined, non-resident alien are not words just stamped on my forehead. Unless amnesia is a non-existent word in your heritage dictionary. And then, there was once upon a time, a time engineered for the flow of forced horse-shoe blue bloods, and pedigrees who turned amnesiac soon after. I left the blue blood of my pedigree sitting lonely at erstwhile airport terminal when I arrived disapproved and stamped, fresh off the boat. An FOB. Gucci, Prada, Vera Wang, Dolce Gabbana, Oscar de la Renta, you yourself now hyphenated, you regurgitate pedigree names forgetting you-are-of-a-massive accretion. And the molten lava still gurgles in the pit spewing reality on your artificial, genetically engineered, amnesic illness. Please don't give amnesia a bad name. It's real for some. And I don't wait for you to call me anything. I do it myself. Brown, dark, woman, single mother, of color, an accent, and sometimes ethnic clothes to give you the opportunity to call me queen. Sorry, I refused to bring the snake charmers and elephants patrolling my native streets. Sorry, I refused to bring the snake charmers and elephants patrolling my native streets. They only exist in your catatonic imagination.

Feeling down, being down

Of two downs, this is a tale. Feeling down. Being down. It's the 21st century, hope using the word, down, or period, isn't offensive. It's not offensive when blood from the same body creates life. And neither should feeling down be considered anything more than a human need expressed in reality. Tsunami of a big city's seductiveness appropriates the less strong. And the yin-yang of human sensibilities get thrown around like bloated rubber advertisements. Appropriateness, is it a big city problem? Small suburban hideouts, and tiny rural cutaways, immune to the pulls of dog-eat-dog puppetry? Folks feel down, very down in the hustle and bustle of lights. Lights are glossy and prancing. Hearts and bodies are lonesome, and unobtrusive. Then there were those who vilified a young woman for running the London marathon on the first day of her period. Twenty-six point two miles with the natural narrative of a body feminine dripping in mettle and acceptance. The aching, bloating, grumpy forgotten period of my yester years runs along old chambers of my memory logs, I smile and exhale. Normally, I would rather keep the tell-tale signs private, yet, making a point is what the young woman did. Whether you like it or not, she left behind the female body's raw legacy. This portends freedom, of a kind. Ending of the period, is another kind. Please, don't make a big deal. It's just the freedom from that blood, those cramps, that pain, and that mark in the back of a skirt where a friend spilled ink to hide, to save shame from shaming you and me. City gloss or street incandescent, any or all lights can bring someone down. And a woman can be down, anytime. The statue of liberty is a woman yet women's bodies, thoughts, ideas, actions, are not free from abuse. And, being abused is not the prerogative of women alone. Or, by men, only.

Family blood

As I drove down route X at earlier than six am on the side not whereof my car, lay a white sheet protruding upwards by itself, stationery, forlorn, unclaimed. Flashing police cars raced. My heart palpitated fast. And it seemed all cars on my side were slowing, gliding, perhaps wondering why a blank bulging cloth lay solitary. Had no one yet in this baffling, maddening, desolate world, said, that is my own. For now, just the road to it lay claim. At first, I anticipated it was a poor deer. Poor deer. Poor, poor, deer, not thinking about the poor deer's family. But a blocked highway for miles could not be for an animal, right? Where was the damaged car? Or cars? Other people? Ambulance? I wasn't sure for whom my prayers were, human or deer? Hurt inside was grave as the protruding white sheet seemed dismissed, like I had done a deer, simply calling it, *poor.* And then, humans scorn even their living own.

Democracy in decline

It's not the here-there cavernous potholes, nor the sometimes-dawdling services, not even the sometimes third-world-like public utilities. It's the homelessness and from diseases folks dying in the *first of the first* world, that confounds. There are clear cyphers, all around, this proud democracy is in decline. He walked in with very loose, smudgy pants, halfway down his behind. Had no underwear. Only a big, torn, muddied blanket trying to cover himself. His downward eyes, his dim murmur for coffee at the counter, his not looking at anyone, his incoherent mutterings, talking with himself, constant coughing sent me spiraling into indescribable gloom. Outside, a young woman was holding a sign...

> There is something wrong with America
> Where food and health care are privileges
> And owning guns is a right!

Koala and judases

Mean, mean people slowly unwrap like sundry snake skins. I welcomed them so I hold culpability. They slither away leaving me to create, tend, love, rear a new skin, over and over. Judases. The forest is desiccated and fragile. Perfect for a fire. And I don't smoke. I see your smoky footprints in my backyard, sore and fiery, leaving me to douse these with my own skin, my own fabrics, my own rush, over and over. See my skin, my bark, my leaves, my tiny legs heaped in layers on the sun's anchor. Judases. I see wisdom knocking on my door, solidly, repetitively. I see the residues from rampant wildfires spill just outside my abode. I see you and others cooking on those very dangerous embers. Judases. I don't watch. I observe. I look pointedly. That's my job. Like the Gods of all religions observing us. I may look short and cute, yet I thrive on tall Eucalyptus that your pettiness can never reach. Unless you burn the trees. I can live long except for your foolhardiness that lights a match or pulls along in old, smelly rags your diseases with the intent to devastate and kill. I'm forced to be your sins. Your narcissism. Your juvenile behavior protruding like Pinocchio's nose. Judases.

The above poem was inspired by work of Australian poet, writer, painter, and sculptor, Elizabeth 'Lish' Škec

Babylon, my sinful dance muse

I found it one day, searching for a place to learn line dancing, in Northern Virginia suburbs just a footstep from my beloved Washington DC. I did more than learn. I danced. I loved. I lost. I pined. Felt it all. My sinful dance muse, Babylon, where I could let go with no one to judge me, except me. A glass of champagne or two serenaded, along with many men who wanted to know where I was from, accentuating in baritone, *"you are so exotic,"* while shaking hands with their middle finger caressing my palm just so swiftly, innocuously. Came to know later they were testing if I was up for a one-night stand. No man! Go find another loser! The club grew on me as did its men.Most women there became sisters of convenience. My sinful love, Babylon with low lights, hookahs and cigars, Go-Go bands, DJ and club music, food and spirits plenty. And the dance floor was like my bed that I could make love on with the man of my fantasies without any *desi* pointing a finger. *"Hey, you...have you gone mad! A woman with a grown-up son, dancing in mini dresses late at night, drinking booze in those cheesy American clubs instead of prostrating before Hindu Gods praying for peaceful old age!"* Babylon, thank you, for being my sinful dance muse.

*Desi: People native to India, indigenous

Pity, go take a hike

A square shape marked the spot at which it sat in the "museum collection" my parents jokingly called the old, seventies record players cupboard. My lips blew off the dust that stubbornly settled back on my face. Relentless, I put on a vinyl by the iconic group, No Losers.

"Pity, go take a hike
Go take a hike
A hike my man, a hike you take
No time to waste after the wake
It's not gonna be me on the merry go round
My honey's missing on the turn around
So, Pity, go take a hike, go take a hike
Even if it's on a bike
Don't come back to me
Till you are a mature tree, or better still, never to be
Pity, go take a hike
Go take a hike
A hike, my man, a hike you take
No time to waste after the wake..."

That song was blaring when Pity stopped by the other day. Sometimes it wakes up and starts jogging at odd times. Knocking at my door, at odd times. Doesn't sleep when it should. *"Don't should me,"* said Pity angrily at me. *"What's got you so upset?"* I asked gently putting my arm around its slouching shoulders. *"You aren't disappointed in me, are you, just because I don't say hi?"* Pity heaved, shook its feeble head and walked away, without a word. The rock it was sitting upon was cold, and the wind around it frozen. Birds were perched soundlessly, and trees were hanging upside down. But the fragrance of the classic old rose puffed itself down my nostrils. I took a long *Pranayama* breath and let it go, glazing the transparent ice in front. As I wiped the haze, my fingers warming to an uplifted spirit, I saw chocolate ice cream, peanut butter cookies, some Indian rice pudding, and other sugar heavies all vying to set the table. *"Hurry up, hurry, it's been too long..."* they called for me. *"Come before the moment of healing passes."* I wasn't really dressed for company. Nor did I feel like changing, nor stuffing myself with too many sweeties. Their pleadings grew boisterous, and grabbing my slippers, I ran out in my PJs, away from candied sugar coatings to a different healing. Duplicitous pity no longer getting away with games. I had churned me some meditation as I hummed along

"Pity, go take a hike
Go take a hike
A hike my man, a hike you take
No time to waste after the wake
It's not gonna be me on the merry go round
My honey's missing on the turn around
So, Pity, go take a hike, go take a hike
Even if it's on a bike
Don't come back to me
Till you are a mature tree, or better still, never to be
Pity, go take a hike
Go take a hike
A hike, my man, a hike you take
No time to waste after the wake..."

*Pranayama: Yogic practice of focusing on breath

Finally, I showered

The bed was taciturn and neatly spread with arms inviting, and I wanted to sink into the muslin covers. Wanting to have a drink first and shower, I turned the water on, waiting for the right temperature. My son had got married today. Twenty years after we'd left India. As I aged, alchemists tugged at my sleeves often. And wanderers and travelers gestured to me, come join us in your years of autumn with graying hair at your temples, graying all over. The aging, hopefully maturing my restless travels, my restless needs, my desires and wants now quietly straddling the times. No more pseudo agendas written by some men. No more equality diminishing. No more pendulum shaking Zen. No more sham standards lowering or raising. Why some men slouch on recliners, beer in hands? Why then they unbuckle their belt, zip open their pants? Why don't such exhibitions come from women? Are fertility eggs stronger than tasteless semen? Is exhaustion an excuse from housework? Seems their power steam tends to be on steroids. Men need to learn more about their tools before smearing those who learn to swim in the shallowest of water pools. I called my thoughts to come home like wandering sheep back to the pen and reflected on the last time I made love. The baggage accrued in life seemed to weigh me down and also allure me to freedom. Letting my *lehenga* fall I checked my breasts for any signs of a lump. A deep sigh filled under the steaming water as I finally showered.

*Lehenga: Indian ethnic dress

Portions of this poem are from onegin stanzas in the author's unpublished novel

Covid19's inverted triangle

When sadness seizes and piles and piles on to Covid19's lunatic inverted triangle. When murders, accidents, rapes, war, suicide, civil conflicts, law and order losses, and untold diseases vie for double jeopardy during that very Covid19's irrationality. When mortgages lay peeved in vaults. When vaults are empty. When homes are fumigated. When poor are dehumanized. When animals are terminated. When nature is brutalized. When a synthetic world churns and churns and churns, with life at the mercy of a seething gale gone intractable. Then, then, I'm the hug that most may never feel again. I'm the knee most are begging on to spare their loved ones. I'm the beam, giggle, joke, tease, exclamation, question, shout, climax, scream, run, birth, walk, sleep, that are lost in the ringing of secluded deaths. Why God, why? Where's this anger, disdain, discarding of your creations on Earth coming from? What sins, wrongs, arrogance, disrespect did we knowingly or unknowingly commit? Why am I questioning you, God? Narcist humans' experiment, misuse, abuse, violate any and all species on Earth. You must be sick of us, God, and turned the life triangle upside down. As I lay in bed each night, my prayers are for my children and millions in the rotting inverted triangle. Later, I turn and lay on my stomach, my eyes dampening the bedsheet as thoughts of not having someone spoon me again mist my heart. Love is even more ephemeral now. Where are those who vilified karmic cycles with their vulgar chants, *"Money, power, money, I have millions/I don't need you and you and you/Go live in your cheap pavilions."* Can they turn the inverted triangle around? Can love turn humanity around? Can a new base be built? So, God can rest for a while & also us

Who let the pigs out?

Who let the pigs out?
You? You? Or you?
Who let the pigs out?
You? You? Or you?
And then they came in throngs, malodourous and burping, and uttering some gibberish. They walked the alley ways, walked the staircase, walked the hallways, walked in their mind's ways, walked in their caved nostrils, walked with their shady tails. Marching in heavy and thick bison hide boots, dragging them pigs by loose knotty shoestrings and misconstrued words that they barked out like half pigs and half dogs. Their stenches were sitting on their heads, somersaulting in their uncombed hair, carrying tiny shovels and hay picks which they'd shove into the skins of them pigs to bolster any slow in the blitz. Far away, beyond the outskirts of decency, neon billboards had manicured and flashy nail polished hands, promoting, squawking like town criers, cheap hairbrushes in fluorescents. The pigs winked at the tempting hands exchanging crummy text messages:
We let the pigs out
We, we, we!
We let the pigs out
We, we, we!

Tequila and spice memories

The storms inside at times are hushed, at times vocal, at times fictional, at times like a memoir urging me to tell all as one would after a couple of Tequila shots. Neat. Untailored. Maybe a bit abridged as my giggles roll in free fall like tiny diamonds on the loose, that my dog tries to swallow as I force her to spit them. Who is going to catch the mysticism of punditayans, fakirs, gypsies, hippies, fairies, pixies, and dervishes in the glinting glass pieces of my life? Revolving, oscillating, gamboling, they murmur my tale in snippets as they vie to reach the end of the hopscotch of my reminiscences, contemplating which recollections to retrieve from hand stitched dress pockets. From New Delhi to America holding my son's little hand, I mapped, and I trekked. Reels and reels of happenings, instances, episodes, moments that I rolled on my fingertips, even pleated, and clutched and embraced. Owned. Professed. Conceded. Some, I disputed. And laid the admitted neatly, one on top of another like my Indian shawls and saris in cedarwood drawers I bought at flea markets in Virginia suburbs. Mustiness of spices and Fall leaves mingled to create original, unmarked fragrances, new retentions. Every now and then, I recline observing life as I have a couple of tequila shots and hold my tongue on the stories I tell.

*Punditayans: Female for the word, pundits *Fakirs: Muslim or Hindu religious ascetic or mendicant monks *Dervishes: Members of a Muslim religious order noted for devotional exercises, especially dancing in circles

Blues of a resilient Indian woman in mid-America small town

A fall. That accident no one saw coming. Those bones that cracked. My mom's sister's. Nearing ninety and like all our family women, tenacious strength kept her alive, asserting on a load of fascinations, sometimes not bountiful. Like that day on pruning the creepers on top of the back-porch pergola. *"I could have done it."* She echoed intractably later. A loud thud, a yell and immobilization followed. And malaise followed me as I rushed with loads of junk snacks, with my kind mother's soul keeping me company. Over six hours drive. Numerous fears of corona days filled me, but I just kept driving and driving. On a mission, my mask handy. Her house lay barren and purposeless, and the step stool lay solemn, eyeing me in guilt. *"How much was it you?"* I asked the mayhem. A potted plant thriving with flowers lay on its side just as I imagined she did. It was raining intensely; the wind was blowing aimlessly. The scene seemed clueless as I took a remembrance picture of a resilient Indian woman having another of her blues in between some greens and yellows too. Sixty years since she drove into that tiny place, with one street downtown in the middle of nowhere America thousands of miles from somewhere India. All over the house a kind of dripping cultural odor followed me. I touched her ethnic collections in well-planned rooms trying to sense her resolutions, and mine. Photographs, wall hangings, cushions, papier-mâché dolls, baskets. My hands lingered on most everything, principally on her scrawled notes found everywhere, even in old magazines. Like I stumbled upon my mom's after she passed in New Delhi. Yes, I have the blues too. Yes, I fall even without the treacherous step stool. And, yes, I brave it out too. Flick away the blues, like flicking away a breeze disturbed curtain caressing my cheeks in the night slumber. Or a fly in a car on a fast speed highway. A lot of flicking going on by resilient Indian women on the move.

King is not well

Polished floors, closed doors, clean ceilings, and patched windows stare at the raped halls. Raped halls. People ran, dirty feet pilfering. Then came, the disjointed band. Legs up-down, up-down. Arms stiff-up-sideways, stiff-up-sideways. Hollering, bellowing lies. Megaphones being charged with diesel generators inside soon-to-be culpable throats. Throats that are so dehydrated they can't stop sipping water from huge non-recyclable bottles. Bottles that echo back human noises and add to the planet's waste. Crude and intimidating. Unwise injunctions mandating. And the solon of environment squatting cross-legged on bruised, panting skin, cringes, shifting its body weight to ease the pressure on ancient bodies. In thick haze lies the kingdom. The king is not well. Subjects remind him of glorious days. Sometimes he grins, sometimes he waggles. Subjects staunchly pray to the Gods. *"Take his pain away, let him walk again. Let him eat, croon, cavort and rule again."* But the subjects are in deep fight. Squabbles are in open sight. They will not find a solution till rid of self-promotion. Drop the power game. Throw the dice in the drain. The world is ablaze, and untimely ghosts are out seeking victims. They question the mock pride of kings, nobles, clans and ordinary folks who are now like demons. There seems to be no absolute truth except humankind torturing their own. Seeds of hate sown. Legs up-down, up-down, arms stiff-up-sideways, stiff-up-sideways parade down the obstruse streets, nails strewn across the cold tar. No blood oozes. They've steeled themselves. The king no one refuses.

Teaching chair yoga at an assisted living home

Before Covid19 belted, every week I would go, twice. I felt a bit gloomy, and would often sit in my car later, letting it out. For old age. For Dementia. For Alzheimer's that grip many. Or just the Western system of older folks living in assisted living homes. Where were their families? Did they not want them? Was this individualism? My Indian upbringing and culture would keep nagging. Every week, I took the elevator to the third floor, and my concerns heightened. The room was mostly shushed, though television game channels blurted out occasional automated hoots. No one really reacted. I'd say hello, optimistically. Some beginning to recognize would get up to give me a welcoming hug. It felt soothing. Putting on some relaxing music I'd urge. Urge. And urge, like a mother to her reticent children. Urge them to do what I was doing, follow my directions, my entreaties, my cheerfulness, my steps. Some repeated agreeably. Some chortled like naughty kids at a game they were eager to play. Some walked around without stopping. Some sat transfixed. Some looked through me. Some ignored, turning their head anticipating any minute their loved ones to come walking down the hallway. Some checked their cell phones oft. Some explained they were waiting to be picked up, taken out for lunch. A movie. Or back home. Then Covid19 came along reminding harshly everyone is on the same journey. Searching for home which isn't the mad walls of manipulation. Not the fanatical voices of terror. Not the fury, roars, bawling, aghast darting footsteps, the hands raised in "don't shoot me, please." At the assisted living home, among the very elderly, among those with their memory diminishing, not able to connect the dots and lines in their brain too well, I knew I was among those who'd seen and lived life.

Chair Yoga: An adaptation of traditional yoga, done sitting on a chair
Namaste: A form of greeting in India

A new day

Clap, clap, clap. The sky is ablaze with lighted hands clapping. An equal number of feet join the tango and there is no need for radio or television. Covid19 seems trapped in some boils and squares or rectangles. Everywhere else stillness seems to be prevailing. I finally wear my gold sheer stilettoes, a sweater dress in scarlet, matching gloss on my lips, a clutch in gold, and go out. I see cubes driving cars and cars are circles. Buildings are thin and upright into the clouds, and grass is grown on threadlike reeds. Many hued shops and neon signs gesture with a forefinger pointing at us from restaurant tops. Rest is hidden, cut by titanic scissors that hang from the sky. I see myself and you as two tiny shadows between the ridges and ache to touch. The music is loud, and you are not there in flesh to pirouette with me. I am alone in all the spheres and keep spinning in a trance that seems to go on forever. I run helter-skelter, opening all the doors till I see my bed. I don't waste time and let no haunts visit my dreams either. Next morning is crisp like a newly plucked orange and as I sip the juice, the phone rings. *"Corona took him."* Residue of the second shot in my arm aches but it's a new day.

The above poem was inspired by the work of Canadian mixed media artist, Lorette C. Luzajic

Ancient creation (just one small perspective)

Who am I to say how we humans were created? Biology, aliens, God or mythical writings passed from generation to generation defining untold lens theology. We spooned, we boomed, we zoomed. Who am I to say from where I came? Or you. Or them. Or any identity chosen or shoved upon us. I do know, I do know, I'm wood encasing a soul, best I can. Oud, ancient agarwood of a woman escaped from mutilated identities. Not here to create new ones. Legends, birth, rebirth marry my soul. And the clothes, hairstyle, lipstick are whiffs of a sweet patina with which I lacquer my naked self. You'll need to sift beneath the apparent grains, if you wish to find me. Go through the trials with me. More I age, more with ease I stand. I'm a blue lunar drink. Stirred. On the rocks. Peppery. I'm just fine kindling that my sins, and yours, tried not to decay so I could wrap my soul, and yours, tenderly. I do know many other matters of head and heart. The movement, the veers, the tilts, the growth, the hiatus, the gales, the peace one hopes would engulf the human race shedding all contrived constructs. Creation can be divisive, excessive, avoidable. Or, unifiable, sufficient and enjoyable. Who decides? I do know. I do know, I'm a long itinerant spirit. I culminate in one birth and regerminate in another, and another, millions within me call out, glow, bellow and make love. In every life, every dimension, every cosmos, every microscopic piece of information or dna left behind. Who will accept? I do know, do know, I carry within me the silver of distant specks, the blades of archaic hidings, the luminosity of free bodies and the blushes of unpretentious raptures. Of being. Of goodness reaped. Of goodness fostered frequently after falling in the muck, my own and that of yours. Who will see? I do know, I do know the tincture I've prepared so carefully and thoughtfully from icy and molten nectars, rainbows, stars, planets, meteors, comets and all that I could not see and did not know. I blindfolded myself so I would not be biased against any of my children.

Kali asks, Two, three, repeated or karmic wrongs make a right?

I am woken in the middle of the night by nightmares of infernos gulping homes, smoke rising and rising, nowhere to go. I am woken up in the middle of the night by the squeals of tornadoes and tempests volleying up their impenetrable bodies against weaker souls. I am woken up by whispers, innuendoes, pleas and gasps. Woken up by jolts of human tongues spitting out the most punitive words, to demean, to deride, to kill. Two wrongs, three wrongs, repeated wrongs, karmic wrongs, the loop keeps looping. No one to pull, reign in, or break the cursed circle to commence afresh. My skin scalds, my skin corrugates, my skin festers. I don't give up. I am *Kali* and *Parvati,* and I am dark and a goddess too. I can control time. Alter time. Make time difficult for you. Take you away from time. I am magnificent. I forgive. I have streaming passion that is filled with *Shiva's Tandavam.* He may lay at my feet. May seem in obeyance. May seem asleep on purpose. Mistake not, he's very aware. Maybe in awe, in veneration, of my *Shakti,* my ardor that fills him. Rouses and arouses him. Keeps him guessing. I am modern. I am a traditionalist. I destroy. I love. And I make love in all my forms and moods. And I am just. I am benign. I see much more subterranean than my third eye. I scrabble the third often to make sure no scrap of learning is left untouched. I may not fully understand each entry in my brain cells. But I seek it. Let it rest in the sun. Marinate. Not curdle. I caress it. I prod it. I hope that humans can feel it too. I am a female Goddess just imparting, unscrupulously, what's circulating in my frame.

*Kali: Goddess of protector against evil *Parvati: Goddess of fertility *Shiva: God of destroyer *Tandavam: Cosmic dance performed by Shiva *Shakti: Power

Fallacy of a single, immigrant mom

Single mothering is tough, they say. Being an immigrant is tough, they say. Single immigrant mom or immigrant single mom? Yes, I know folks keep saying, *"Single mothering is tough. Not good for the child. Not good for the parent. There is no father. The child is yateem. And an immigrant too!"* So many societal injunctions. This. That. Comments, comments, comments. Patriarchal mostly, despite being born in the land of myriad female goddesses. The West is not very different. A half-moon reveals a single mom's impending motherhood. The father is not there. Deserted, dead or jailed. Just not there. Durable mamas in most cultures. Father is not questioned when there is no mother. Division and multiplication accolades proliferate on twitter. Leaving deductions and subtractions sifted into a mother's bowl. I did not let that shatter my resolve, wasn't a soft cookie. Nor did my tenacity melt away like overrated margarine on hot toast. I always use real butter. Encouraged my son on similar wavelength. Recent immigrants around me were buying homes, establishing real estate roots, while I was on a journey to raise a decent human being.
"Degrees, degrees, degrees, it's not funny,
It's the status and a rich man's world" (Abba extended)
"Give it up man, decent, decent, decent
I wanna raise a decent human in this snooty world."
Duality of being Indian and American did not stress me out too much. Neither did hyphenated identities keep me awake at night. Nor did nostalgia burrow into me. I did not flatten, singe, or be puffy eyed. Instead, dares of finest integrations of cultures, like trusting and clasping strangers' palms in a robbed night, kept me goading. Folks only saw the tip above the waters for mom and son. We were like Maya Angelou's oil wells were pumping in our living room despite first furniture being hand-me-downs. I am a single, immigrant, pleased, grateful mom. And that's no fallacy.

*Yateem: Orphan

Of in-laws

And so Draupadi's bridal sari was ensconced in a monsoon drizzle of wishful sequins that came sauntering carrying whispers of celebrations and warnings. She held her sari *pallu* high like a flag of defiance. Bedazzles of a neoteric doomed marriage could be heard in the vicinity of the cloaked moon. Draupadi's strides irreverential to the glass of norms and respect her mother-in-law gave her. *"Drink it up, it's hot outside, and you have to satisfy all five of my sons."* The glass fell, rolled off into a painting a pseudo was drawing. Inside the canvas pulled nail splinters became flying feathers, searching for their throbs gone too soon. Draupadi's amusement and caution were seen shaking hands, clumsily, fearfully, rebelliously. Water lay in comatose watching from inside a pottery urn. Cold. Undrunk. Unfelt. Unquenched thirst like the unseen itch of ageless conifer trees, like the hallowed belching of sun laved skies, like the hysterical land beneath a fatigued dam of quicksand. Draupadi was fine gold dust out the time glass. There was no going back and henceforth when she spoke, her body slid through sandglass's tapered waist reappearing as disillusioned morsels of scalding boiled rice which she trundled the same for everyone.

*Pallu: The corner or side of the sari end *Draupadi: The doomed heroine in the Hindu epic, Mahabharata

The above poem was inspired by the work of Australian poet, writer, painter, and sculptor, Elizabeth 'Lish' Škec

Why I usually cry in the shower

When water runs down my bare skin. Just water on me. Running down my head, hair, face, neck, and on the twists, bends, bulges, and crevices, down till they reach my toes, winding their way through each one of em, and onto the floor where water collects, huddles for a while like winter cold around a bonfire, sharing stories of body parts they'd just wetted and then gaily they skitter down the drain like a cluster of loose rubies, then, and then, when nothing rests between water and me, I usually cry. Maybe some soap lies between us. Maybe some undies I need to wash. Maybe some of my body parts I still need to clean. But after all is done, and it's just me, the water and my porous casing, I usually cry. A lot. The yearning comes not from where my heart resides. I've learned to coax it. Not from where my thoughts meander. I've learned to hush those. But from somewhere deeper. From that core beneath my spirit, behind my back, under my spine, below the blood where the atoms usually dwell and mingle. I cry for lost opportunities, lost relationships, status, family jamborees, cultural sustenance, lost growing romantic-old together, lost years of youth, lost newsflashes and lost sentiments that refuse to let go and sink with the soapy aventurines. After my tears have been fully pulled out, drained, syphoned, and dried, then I become tranquil, and gratefulness fills my heart. Not everyone has everything. If I have to go through the same all over, in another life, I'll accept it as long as in each timeframe my child is born to me again.

Gandhi's *chaadar*

Gandhi's *chaadar* was soiled. From agony, loss, and it was weighted, demoralized, dripping with howls of humans kicked, beaten, violated, deserted, forsaken. Millions of *chaadars* soiled from India to Pakistan, Pakistan to India. One nation, two hearts beginning to beat their own drums at a very soiled hour. My *chaadar* is not soiled. Not soiled. Not soiled. Like those of my parents. Like those of millions unknown. Like that of Gandhi's. My *chaadar* is not soiled. Not soiled with blood, bones, limbs and tears from movement, migration, displacement. From scuttling, begging to be left alive. I am grateful. Grateful for sacrifices that make me stand tall and free today. My heart bows. My mind reflects. My soul is humbled at the relentless march from India to Pakistan, Pakistan to India. One nation, two hearts beginning to beat their own drums at a very soiled hour. Numerous old philosophies Gandhi carried in a knot at one end of his *chaadar,* unwound to woo the masses at timed moments. *Satyagraha* and *Ahimsa,* not new, but repositioned in the political world. To impel, attract Indians. To confound, exasperate the British. With a *chaadar* and a small loin cloth, an ingenuous man circumstances created, a compelling man events dictated. My *chaadar* shudders from harrowing pressures of his conclusions, choices, and of people without choice from India to Pakistan, Pakistan to India. One nation, two hearts beginning to beat their own drums at a very soiled hour.

*Chaadar: Bedsheet/wrap *Satyagraha: Truth *Ahimsa: Non-violence

Snoot & snout

Snoot. Snout. More snoot. More snout. Where's the tissue! Snobbishness of towering buildings claiming touching the skies. For whom? Mighty organizations claiming reaching the clouds. For whom? Silk suited and booted with bison hide briefcases claiming being rushed. For whom? Immaculate manicured hands flashing plastic money claiming business. For whom? Snoot and snout. Snout or snoot. What difference does it make? It's a lot of snoot and snout darting about, rubbing noses at each other as well. No one's safe in the snoot and snout space. Multi-nationals, medium, small, nonprofits, halls of great learning, the snoot and snout are not just of the richy-richly rich. Coveted degrees, flaunting diplomas. For whom? Spitting jargons, euphemisms, parables and riddles. For whom? Pretentious noses uppity dropping ivy league names. For whom? Snoot and snout. Snout or snoot. What difference does it make? It's a lot of snoot and snout darting about, rubbing noses at each other as well. No one's safe in the snoot and snout space. In my frustrated daydreams, I speak often with my mother. Sitting in the open courtyard of our ancestral home, she'd be wiping her sweat off by the corner of her sari. Judiciously surveying a veranda large enough to hug the rooms and makeshift kitchen gardens sprouting edibles, she'll call out. *"Hey, beta, come here na. The coconut oil will harden."* Barefoot I'd run, my teenage years animated, and I'd plump down on the floor, my frock flying. She'd oil and comb my hair every weekend, speaking ever so softly not to disturb my moon flirting, slipping in sensible aphorisms that in my silver years tip toe into the rooms of my consciousness when the snoot and snout attempt to invade my peaceful reflections. Snoot and snout. Snout or snoot. What difference does it make? It's a lot of snoot and snout darting about, rubbing noses at each other as well. No one's safe in the snoot and snout space.

*Na: A word used to stress upon something *Beta: Hindi word for child

Hope

Who is that standing at the foot of the hill? Who is that chanting? Is that Hope, influenced by Martin Luther King's 1968, crisp, rejuvenating, optimism-filled Spring April speech in Memphis, Tennessee? But wait, no one is listening. Martin said, *"Well, I don't know what will happen now. We've got some difficult days ahead. But it really doesn't matter with me now because I've been to the mountaintop...and I've seen the Promised Land. I may not get there with you. But I want you to know tonight, that we, as a people, will get to the Promised Land!"* Hope gasps, stops chanting, falls to the knees, forehead knotted, eyes pinching with unfulfilled aspirations. No one else is there on the desolate hill. No one. Still. Hollow. Desperate, deeply depressed, Hope sits dejected, all alone in the blank night. If no one comes out to listen, this word will have no meaning soon. Differences that made us unique now yell for sadistic, rabble-rousing. And graveyards, cremation grounds or Towers of Silence are flooded with sniffles of innocents gone after an embryonic existence only. "Hope, get up, get up, please, stand up, start speaking again. See, there is Martin, on the hill, with his outstretched hand. And see, Gandhi and Mandela are there too, seeking you. Get up Hope, there is still time, there is still time, for some to understand your meaning. Get up, speak, chant again, and again, and again. Please don't let demagoguery pull you into an unrelenting abyss."

Blame

Blame resides in picking. Picking of alternatives, and the specificity of the right instance. And instances have the propensity to switch, twitch, twist, turn, vault. Pickings can be sticky, and stickiness can be by optional picking. Yesterday I was there thinking of how it would be here. Today I am here thinking of how it was there. No one told us in childhood that desires and well chalked out plans can get caught in the mesh of time, space, and matter. Moby Dick chops off many an Ahab's leg, and many Moby Dick aren't lucky. Or Ahab. Perception. Perception is not reality as there is no one reality. I can enter the storm anytime, and like a flying potter, create, create, and create anew. Surely, I will change in the storm, and you'll blame me for changing on you. I'll blame you for letting me go so easily. Unknown to you, you are still in your own raging storm, one that you created having tea one day in a picturesque non-native roadside café in a world we knew not much about like the new planet X just beyond disowned Pluto. We believed all you told us. Belief and blame can be ignorant bed partners. Blame is sitting on the matted daybed outside in the sunny courtyard now, fanning itself. It asks for cold water. As I hand over the glass, it manages a crooked smile and whispers, *"you all keep fighting while I bask in the glory of your missed opportunities."*

I interpret my colorless drink

Pour yourself some scotch. Pour yourself some water. Pour yourself some erudition from the *Tree of Souls,* and I'll listen. Pour yourself some ire, some envy, some conceit, and I'll stare at you enough to freeze you down. Don't be fooled by my Prada tailored suit. The devil's been walking at the edges and I'm quite industrial in my taste and interpretive of your musings, including me. Paintings resting against raw, textured, unprepared walls set the tenor and windows as tall as in airplane hangars alight the ambiance. So, please, pour yourself some scotch. Pour yourself some water. Pour yourself some erudition from the *Tree of Souls,* and I'll listen. Pour yourself some ire, some envy, some conceit, and I'll stare at you enough to freeze you down. I'm a nyctophile and aurora. I'm the stream of consciousness and I often sit in vacant chairs in banter with uncountable, unbeknownst minted ideas. I aint got much time. No one got much time. I aint unique. No one's unique. I aint above board. No one's above board. Yet this is as interpretive as I can get that when the song returns dragging its over used legs, I'm the one to run out, apologizing for sending it out too many times. I move around, rummaging for some salve, before finding my way back to the main. Friends become acquaintances and the latter just stop being anything. The pandemic could be blamed if you wish. I still want to remain the light's blessing so blaming an illness makes not for a good white lie. So, please, pour yourself some scotch. Pour yourself some erudition from the *Tree of Souls,* and I'll listen. Pour yourself some ire, some envy, some conceit, and I'll stare at you enough to freeze you down.

*Tree of Souls is the name of the sacred tree for the Na-vi people in the movie Avatar

The above poem was inspired by the work of New Jersey, USA based graphite pencil artist, Anthony Gartmond

Rape

It's my body, not yours. It's my body, not yours. You pilfer Mother Earth when you pilfer me. You pilfer the country when you pilfer me. You pilfer yourself. Your future. Your karma. Your mother, sister, wife, daughter, when you pilfer, violate, pillage, rape me. When you pilfer me, you pilfer all the female goddesses you pray for wealth, safety, learning and good fortune. And then you carry the hypocrisy of your worship on your weak, scheming, dishonest, unmanly shoulders to the alley, the dark alley, or to the dark buses, or the dark trains, or the dark fields, or even entering homes in the dark, where you hunt, grab, muffle, force. And then you walk away from a cold, naked, bloodied dead soul that refuses to leave, sits outside the body, weeping, ashamed, broken, void, incensed. *Nirbhaya, Unnao, Kathua, Shakti Mills, Hathras, Balrampur, Hyderabad.* Remember. Remember the names. Thousands more countless, faceless. It you don't remember the names, remember a woman's body, a young girl's body, a female child's body raped and dumped like it was not life. They say they are deprived. The ones that commit the crime. They say they aren't reared well. The ones that commit the crime. Products of crowded homes, poor homes. No sex education. Mystification of a woman's body in Bollywood movies. Excuses, excuses, excuses. Why do parents not teach their sons that another human body is as important and sacred as theirs? Period. Full stop. You shall not touch by force. Not touch without consent. Not touch when repelled. Not touch when your puny, sick manly ego is bruised. She cried. She cried. She cried. She ran. She ran. She ran. She kicked. She kicked. She kicked. He raped. They raped. And then the maniac in them multiplied, and slashed, and slayed. Even Incubus in hell will not take their dirty, dirty souls.

*Nirbhaya, Unnao, Kathua, Shakti Mills, Hathras, Balrampur, Hyderabad: Fictitious names given to women or real names of places where horrific rapes have occurred in recent times in India

I did not say, *I love you,* to my mama

It had drizzled that morning and the soil was still damp as my son and I took the Uber to the hospital. New Delhi is very earthy when it rains. Unpretentious, it strolls into one's heart and settles in a hug next to your soul. Its fragrances blossom and its smells, its traffic nuisances, its busy body-ness, its capital city pretentiousness, recedes. The vibes change from testiness to serene. This time the tranquility transmogrified into unnerving. I had this feeling this would be the last time I would see my mother alive. She lay on the hospital bed, no movement. Complaining was not her habit in any case. Cancer had spread rapidly in a matter of two months. She opened her eyes on hearing our footsteps. *"Can you take me to the bathroom?"* The care worker got up in reflex. *"No, not you, my daughter will take me."* She looked at the unruly hair strands falling from her bun in the mirror after washing. *"You are so beautiful, mummy."* I muttered. She smiled and we both sat on the windowsill for a while. I just holding her. Later, I held on to her real close that evening before rushing to the airport to catch our flight back. She looked directly into my eyes right through to my inner being. This is it. This is goodbye my darling she seemed to express. Laying on the bed, other relatives watching, she couldn't say anything more. *"We will return very soon, mama."* I whispered as I kissed her on her forehead. At the elevator door, I said, *"I think I did not say, I love you to her."* You did, you did, others consoled. In the lobby downstairs, I ran into some relatives, *"I think I did not say, I love you to her."* My son comforted me, *"You did, you did."* Before entering the Uber, I turned and looked my mother's way, *"I think I did not say, I love you to her."* *"You did, mama, you did."* As the plane left the tarmac with a distraught drizzle still engulfing New Delhi, my uncontrollable tear drops felt an incomprehensible barrenness. I think I did not say, *I love you,* to my mama.

Bandit queen, *Phoolan Devi*

While I was growing up safe, she was incessantly being battered. I did not know her, but her tales carried far. On a train journey through the *Chambal* ravines where she and her dacoit gang hid, I could sense her tortured yet fighter soul. The ravines seemed like skin that had never been moisturized. And her voice was that bucket in a depleted well gnawing to keep digging for water. It was brutal when a girl child of mere eleven was married off to a man three times her age. Brutal when he molested her. Brutal when her parents rejected her. Brutal when she had to return to her husband. Brutal when she was raped multiple times. Brutal when she decided to become a bandit. Brutal when she chose revenge and killed many in return. Brutal when the men she loved were killed. Brutal when she spent many years in jail. Brutal she was assassinated after rebuilding her life. Commodified, from birth to death. A woman can be underrated like bamboo sticks that hold immense weight in muddy backwater canals. Or can be blown out of proportion like tsunamis unable to comprehend they are best thriving in arcane waters. Phoolan Devi, a mix of the two, never resting, showing her middle finger to brutality.

*Phoolan Devi (1963–2001) was a woman of a "lower caste" from a small village in the state of Uttar Pradesh *Chambal: Name of a river that flows through the states of Madhya Pradesh and Rajasthan in India

Jazz vocalist

Smooth jazz flows through me, supple, tantalizing, experimenting like a clairvoyant searching, yearning, transforming bereaved into lived again. There's an ocean streaming through the club where I'm performing, and the Middle Passage is inflamed. All around ancestors are beating their chests. Unnerving howls are unable to break the chains. Burnt rose buds flutter yowling my saga wondering how they'd survive infancy. You, and you, and you, or even you, may not fully get it. The syrupy fragrance and the rips fusing in my veins. Don't ask me whose fault it is. Delve your arms into your belly for that gut of yours. Pull it out. Shake it. Awake now. Ask it. Outside its pouring saxophones and hums, echoes, reverberations and also muzzled restlessness. The last is louder than all. Some barrels, some mast, some bullion, some pelt. The other day I went on a fancy cruise to where the slave ships cut through alien waters far, far away from home and the saxophones were enthralling there too. The top deck was brilliant and mopped clean. A little rueful. A bit queasy. And many stood watching the pulse of the ocean in satin and silk dresses and velvet tuxedos. It's raining dead people now. Warmth and hearth are confused.

The above poem was inspired by the work of New Jersey, USA based graphite pencil artist, Anthony Gartmond

Loner walks

My father used to go for long walks, sometimes up to five-ten miles. From our home in New Delhi to wherever his pronouncement prodded him. He'd come back with dinner, and a story or two tell. Of humidity filled skies. Of famished little children exploited by beggar kings similar to the ones in Oliver Twist. Of the food he'd get them while having *chai* at the roadside stall. Of quick chats with shopkeepers. Of auto rickshaws jostling between constricted roads and tapered by-lanes, barely missing people. Of mom and pop small shops. Of how he'd stop outside the five-star hotel on the way debating should he have dinner in an air conditioned stylish décor or use that money to bring home food. Chiding himself for selfish loner thoughts, he'd keep walking past stray dogs, elderly women squatting on *charpoys* or children playing cricket or *kabaddi,* or *kanche,* or *ludo.* He'd come home a bit peevish, his brows folded and arched. He'd bemoan his wife and children never joined him on his loner walks. *"You could have had these eats along the way plus the experience of seeing life."* We'd dash to get plates and mom would hasten to prepare *chai.* Each saw life from our own lens but *chai* made for great interludes. I go for long walks now and I wonder which loner walk has he gone on from which he never returns to tell his stories.

*Chai: Hindi word for tea *Charpoys: traditional bed made of knotted rope on a wooden bed frame *Kabaddi, kanche (marbles) or Ludo (board game): traditional games in India and kabaddi is now an accepted competitive game in the Asian games

And then the pundit asked for my son's father's family name

"Om, om, om…" The fire was burning sharp and picturesque. *"What is your father's surname? Om, om, om…and, from the moon and the sun…. Om…Yes, beta, what's your father's family name?"* The pundit was uttering some worthy words and some that shook me. My inner plight was running around like a teeny irritant mouse without blinking. I'd forgotten to tell pundit to ask my son for my family's name as well. I thought I'd planned it to a T, all the intricate details. Ceremonies like a mapper chalked out. But for silly validation, forgot the paternal family name is still sought after. As a couple walks seven times around the sacred wedding fire, the pundit asks the boy for his father's name. Patriarchal societies still perpetuated. Sitting within jasmine incense and jasmine flowers I rummaged my purse for a tissue. A single mother, I had voyaged for long. Looking around the room, I saw close friends gesturing to let it go. My moist eyes came to rest on the *bandini* tie and dye gold thread embroidered turban sitting proudly on my son's head. I had broken tradition that morning when I'd placed the turban on my son's head. His father stood by without a word. One deep sigh I gave then. One deep sigh I gave now. Outside a gentle wind was blowing ever so graciously as the sound of the auspicious conch rang out, and the sacred ceremonial fire kept an even pace.

*Om: A sacred sound and a spiritual symbol of Hinduism *Bandini: A type of tie-dye textile

Portions of this poem are from onegin stanzas in the author's unpublished novel

Uncertainty, my secret lover

When bulky LED fixtures bumped repeatedly into Edison's wispy incandescent lights; when early morning hungry stray, rabid dogs became the wake-up calls instead of chuckling, clucking cocks, I felt no uncertainty. No uncertainty. No uncertainty in my choices and decisions. Uncertainly became my secret lover, instead, for the smoothest moments when I let it smouch me in the middle of the night, kiss me in the rain wiping tears from my skin, or pour water over me when I bathed with hiccups and quivering not stopping, or unwrap my sari when I slipped naked into my comforter for much needed rest. Uncertainty saw me as is, raw. Uncertainly did not leave me. It remained true, became my secret lover to hold and cherish till death do us part. A lover who was not needy, not pushing and pulling, not commandeering, nor hurling. Uncertainty never raised voices over the humdrum of regularity. I had to tame my lover a bit though like the shrew in Shakespeare's drama. Had to sweet talk, look flirtingly coy when pouting yet, I haven't given away my power to make the calls with certainty when I need to be left alone, to make the imperative preferences and selections. With no fear. No hesitations. No doubts. No uncertainty.

Sri Aurobindo *Ashram*

We stayed at the Sri Aurobindo Ashram in New Delhi for a few days during another of our life's acrimonious debates between right and wrong. These two diametric opposites been sitting on the same scale for many years. The scale was dated and oxidized by the winds of struggle. Who was to adjudicate? Common sense called both to trial. Right kept presenting one argument after another. Wrong pleaded the fifth. Right had a hoarse throat. Wrong was ballooning even more. Marriages can be anomalous. So, child and I sought refuge in New Delhi, before we sought refuge across oceans in America. Didn't have time to offer depression a seat. Or even a quick, off the cuff, absent minded conversation. All we needed was to keep moving. Moving. Moving from ashram, to kid's school, to work, to house hunting, to making sure sanity was always in our pockets, stuffed to the max and zipped up so it wouldn't fall out and vanish in some untraceable address. The Ashram room was stark but cool, food was simple but congenial, and time hung between hopelessness, anxiety and hunger for normal routine. Twenty years later when I look at the Ashram pictures on the net, I see its natural splendor, expansive lawns, gleeful flowers, the alive fountains and pools with floating candles, the yoga classes, a meditative retreat with peacocks traversing the buildings idyllically set back from the main road, away from noise and dust. At that time all I saw was a place we could hide within.

*Ashram: A spiritual monastery, and also a place where travelers can stay for a few days

Airplanes: when a heart came to be in crimson and saffron

I guess, I guess it's tough to say where you are headed. Perhaps away from a love, or to a love. I still have a childlike fascination at you defying gravity. I'm just a relentless romantic so bear me my mushy heart's muse as did Robert Frost whom I met last night as I was making my way for a glimpse of you. He told me to keep walking till I reached a clearing through chunky, concentrated tree tops where the sky and the crimson-saffron mingled with the tints of my cheeks so that I would blush, and a heart would come to be. I stood in the open with arms far above trying to hold on to some magical woodland while shadows of hearts played mischief with my own shadow. Gingerly I tried to clasp them when butterflies flew in from all sides with naughty eyed elves riding abreast. I pinched myself. Shook my clothes and whispered to the heart shadows to come back and they all blushed crimson and saffron, and a heart came to be. I kept watching till I could only hear your hum-clink, and then turned to the elder trees beseeching their imparting. Avatars of all foliage covered me with autumn leaves and my yogic breaths and poses didn't fail as I prepped to fall to rise again. I merged with the terrain with my heart composed as all the crimsons and saffron held arms, and a renewed heart came to be. As you flew out of my sight, I rubbed my eyes watching a paler blue than pale blue sky. Perhaps a lover, or a soldier, a mother or father, or a child are yearning inside you to take them to their loved ones. Your journey is long, yet I'll watch you from my crimson-saffron clearing, my heart next to yours. And when all loved ones have met those waiting, everyone's blushing cheeks will endure, and a heart forever would come to be.

Forgotten musical instruments: No words for our music

As we opened the heavily locked door, a faint smell of mustiness, mothballs and dust wafted our way. And schmaltz. And malaise. My son and I were returning to our home in New Delhi after eons, junctures, chapters. What zeal could I garner from index cards of my memory catalogues? What sentiments would emerge and face me? Query me? Celebrate or denounce me? The sky was cast as was my demeanor. Feeble sun rays were filtering from partially open blind chinks, and my eyes fell on my mom's *sitar* and my violin huddled close together on one side of the study. Encasements of both were decaying at variant intensities. The intact maple frame of the violin uplifted me, and I tapped its neck and chin. The bridge was broken but the sounding post had held. My mom's *sitar* was still wrapped in her *sari*. That's the way she gave it to me. The *sari* was fraying and discoloring but each fold I unwound held fragrances my mom adored. Jasmine *ittar,* L'air du Temps by Nina Ricci. And her own. Still intact was its mahogany body. So was its neck and the main round *kaddu*. Strings of both were rejected, unhinged from their pegs though. I hugged my mom's *sitar.* My son hugged my violin. A chain of respect. No words for our music.

*Sitar: A plucked stringed instrument with origins in India and used in Hindustani classical music *Ittar: an essential oil derived from botanical sources *Kaddu: The main round resonator made of kaddu or Gourd *Sari: Woman's ethnic dress from India

Holika, Sita, Sati

Holika

Fires here, fires there, fires, fires everywhere. Each day, every year, each moment in our minds and hearts too. Fires titanic high and blaring through the comps sounding more ferocious in the pit. Fires on their own mission. Own timeline. To suit some. Some those who walk the halls of respect yet secretly plunder the Earth with fires that fulminate and gash the rainforests. Or any forests. Or street blocks. Or loaded on missiles. On guns and knives, appropriating inhalations, generating infernos. On outcomes twisted, screwed, coiled like thin plastic pipes to suit some. Some those who call for charring their own kith and kin. So, *Holika* burned when she listened to the folly of a man. Why is evil always shown burning, not reforming?

Sita

A God-King's mind disintegrates like contaminated floor joints condemned after a home fire. He bides his queen, *Sita* to walk through fire. Prove her purity, her chastity so his subjects would him respect. False respect like false teeth don't stick for long. And like a glorious dove of honor, Sita emerged from the flames walking straight and poised. No blood shed. No clotting either. No bones powdered into dust. Her sari and face as unruffled as before she entered the fire, willingly, a complacent wife or tending to her own dignity. But her heart was torn to pieces as she feels herself unshielded, exposed. So, marital trust incinerated when a man did not use his sense. Why does a woman only have to walk through fire to prove anything?

Sati

And then the pleading yelps of a woman sacrificed for property or other greed comes from the hollow pit of a blazing wooden mound. Bodies thronged from villages afar to see such a spectacle as if it were a beast effigy shuddering in the flames. They said, a woman must remain unsullied. Let her die with her dead husband. So, an edifice of an immoral shrine came to be. Why does a wife have to sacrifice her life when her husband dies? Fire, fire you test em all. Some you test more, and some small. Women are hoodwinked, coerced, and drugged to sit on you. Why doesn't it rain when you are on you?

*Holika; Sister of the demon king, Hiranyakashipu *Sita: Ram's queen in the Hindu epic Ramayana who is abducted by the demon king Ravana *Sati: A past practice in some parts of Bengal and Rajasthan in India where a wife was supposed to kill herself by self-immolating on her husband's pyre

Maryada and modern *Draupadi*

I am a modern *Draupadi*. No, not with five husbands but could have if I wanted. Polyandry was shoved into me by childhood myths pedestalized by Bollywood. In real life polygamy held the *trishul*. So, don't worry about my *maryada*. You chalk out yours in permanent markers and I will sketch mine in colorful crayons. I can paint castles in the air, I can paint the evergreens, the Himalayas, the Congo Basin, the Great Barrier reef, the Sahara Desert, the Niagara Falls. I can sail at dawn through the Nile, fly at the Canyon at noon, and kiss at the Taj Mahal in the moonlight. Or I can tip toe into your bedroom. Or his and his and his and his. I perspire and perspire, and my ardor heats up and I run for ice holding myself within my own *maryada* before the wetness boils over. I am a modern *Draupadi*. Don't let men dance on my little fingers, nor do I gamble. And spirits only touch my mouth when I am with special lovers. Pure scents on my wrists, behind my ear lobes, swoon me even more as do words of passion and playful banter. I love my curves, my fussiness, my *asanas*, my boogying, my quiet musings, and scribblings, and sleeping skin to sheet. I love your wittiness, smoothness, flavorings like early morning summer rains. I am *Draupadi*'s wishes and yearnings that bring a winter fire's coziness not the scalding of war. Disdain of woman against woman, man against woman, man against man, or anyone against lgbtq, whizzes through the myths reaching me like a hissing coal, and I simmer. And simmer. And simmer, till the heat becomes fiercer and I boil over.
I watch my steps
I watch everybody
I listen to all the footsteps
I may not acknowledge anybody

I learnt from *Draupadi* to reign in my anger
To quieten my hunger
To not leave around temptations
That could shake foundations
Of familial relationships
That as it is, are mired
From decades of squabbles are extremely tired
That I don't bid to push into perpetual eclipses
I want to feel special when I lay down, unforgettable
So, I chose to be me. A woman. Earthy and sensual.

*Draupadi: The doomed heroine in the Hindu epic Mahabharata *Bollywood: Film Industry in India *Trishul: A trident *Maryada: Limit, correctness, moral propriety, proper behavior *Asanas: Yogic poses

There's a hole in my heart but my heart is whole

My head is lowered in prayer. I'm not defeated. Not depressed. Nor barren. There is a hole in my heart, but my heart is not a hole. It's always whole like warm, fresh *rotis* just off the *tava*. Like a spoonful of pure *ghee* in hot lentil curry. Eat, my mom would say, fondly looking into my eyes. That is what a whole is regardless of losses. Like my son patting my head often as I've told him no one's patted my head like that of a child's. That is what a whole is regardless of losses. Yes, my shoulders are slumped. What do you expect after years of hustling? And yes, my eyes are enervated. What do you expect after decades of seeing life in all its fluctuations and vagaries? Still, they look and wait for the nascent visions of youth skipping down the bend of neighborhood and faraway *pardesi* streets. And, yes, still despite childhood scars and youth's splintered hopes, you can see straight through me and beyond into clear skies. The clouds lifting like boiling milk letting tea leaves below be detectible. The hole is empty, but my heart is filled by tiny unquantifiable nuances from those who will always love me. Rest, walk away with concentrated wretchedness sticking to their wagging, admonishing fingertips and pursed lips. Yes, my heart has a hole as wide as my entire torso with my stomach almost mushed up, crunched, forgotten, yet my heart is not a hole that you can pass through anytime. My heart is whole.

*Roti: A flattened round bread from whole wheat flour, like a tortilla *Tava: A flat smooth griddle generally of cast iron on which roti is prepared *Ghee: Pure butter, can be used for cooking or heated and added to food as a last minute taste enhancer *Pardesi: One who lives in a different city or country*

Art gallery prediction

I'd once gone to some big city on a paid sojourn as most conferences end up being. Strangers I'd just met and laughed heartily over wine and cheese accompanied me to observe the thought processes of artists in a gallery. Inside the dimply lit building, one of them held my hand to pull me for a kiss, and I exclaimed in awe at an odd projection crafted with a deck of cards and discarded sashes from carefully wrapped presents. He left with a huff. A mad world I thought. A stuffed crow stood by watching a sparrow sitting daintily on a heart. Was it trying to claim it surreptitiously? Was humanity going barmy? Numbers and alphabets flashed in the yellow fog dominant in the maize that held its own. Plops of paint dripped from cleverly laid brushes resplendent with matte color and an old Olivetti had garbled letters typed on plain paper with stencil cut outs laying on their backs. Balloons of unalike shapes and pigments sat with gapping mouths to catch the dripping paint. Stuffing their tummies, they seemed to grumble of feeling bloated and bouncy. The painting was titled, *a mad world to be.*

The above poem was inspired by the work of Canadian mixed media artist, Lorette C. Luzajic

A window with a view

When it snows (or rains) I sit at my favorite spot to write poetry. My heart feels like a collapsing sandcastle, wet and brackish from Covid19 losses. Legs folded, curled up on the sectional, a side table standing utilitarian with my morning chalice of *chai* latte and some biscuits, I am prepared for the world, and poetry. Seeing the coconutty, cottony snow pouring dense, unremitting and engaged, I easily glide into a stargaze wherein free-floating flakes seem promising. Bone to skin. Salt-sugar to mouth. Lathered cream to earl grey. I feel the crispness and nippiness of granular pearls on my skin, and I hear them falling loose from a slim choker perched daintily on the crochet lace around the neckline of my ivory chiffon kaftan. I pick them up. They are velvety and hot like marshmallows in s'mores above a wintery fire in the gazebo. I see myself cavorting on tiptoes in porcelain teacups stepping carefully on eggshells crafted from alabaster. I feel I'm in a Disney movie and as the reels slide by, I continue to look outside as mesmerizing vignettes pirouette around my meditations. The rice-colored pages of my diary lay unfelt and dry like parchment paper, and I doodle some daisies instead of couplets. My lips curl as I take a linen napkin and wipe the remnants of pleasing ruminations and confectionery iotas and swallow the last sip of frothy *chai*.

*Chai: Hindi word for tea

Educated or enlightened

Two miniature dancers waltz in front of my eyes, in midair trailed by unexceptional confetti. So is a piece of cheesecake and my tongue tries to latch on to delectable taste. I feel upbeat, and the music is subtle, yet promising. Perfumed flowers drift out my nose. Without warning, a burly hand pulls the cake away and my tear ducts drift by like huge snow globes with me inside waving frantically. I rise and try to walk away but step into a giant moat with sticky notes flying like mini tornadoes. Forget it, we aint gonna say sorry, written on each one of them. They gravitate to my body and I am sucked into the vortexes twisting and twisting like thick fabric wringing itself of access water. With a ginormous splash I fall into the moat and slip into unfathomable sleep. I can still hear some men and women magically walking on the water promoting big authors and impressionism, existentialism, surrealism, telling me they were sharing their education, and then they turn around, running away fast, hooting, almost splitting when their hilarity reaches their belly's inner membranes. I can see mushy tissues, skin and veins shaking, almost coughing. A giant incandescent bulb runs after them with me running close behind tugging at the on-off switch. On-off, on-off, on-off. Education whizzes up and sits high on sooty puffs while enlightenment creates a new world in earth, fire, water, wind and ether. The bulb keeps going on-off, on-off, on-off in both worlds, lest either, forget.

The above poem was inspired by the work of Australian poet, writer, painter, and sculptor, Elizabeth 'Lish' Škec

Please don't say he is dead, *Trivia* is possible

What's in a word? Sometimes, it's all in a word. History bears witness. So, please don't say he is dead. Say he has passed away, no longer with us, left us, passed on. *"Please revert the rights of his book to his daughter, the author is dead."* Please don't say that word. Heart pounding, everything in me flooding out, not listening. Hey slow down, it's okay, it's only a word. My hurt is agitated by a word, language as used, stress as laid. Word or not, I know, I can find him no more. If I call his name long and hard enough, my cell might ring with his number popping up. My feet are darting now, don't know where. Stop them, they are too quick, into the cold without socks, seeking chill, moisture or numbed freedom. This season will never change, and seed sods are kind of speechless. Disorganized, chaotic, hoping to land at the station that will take them home. Which home; my home; his home; final home? Is it final there? Where is there? I cannot think beyond the word that slid down my throat like a shaving from a sharpened pencil piercing my esophagus without shame or guilt, echoing inside resolutely. Perhaps I can turn the volume down to prove the word wrong. Or they are wrong who used the word, it rolls right off their tongue. Not thinking, maybe. I close my eyes and see him. I open my eyes and speak with him. Too many doors and windows, unsure of new beginnings or last endings. Leaving a jumbled matrix for *Janus* to resolve or solve. I'm just going to seek *Apollo* to keep singing, repeating things my ears pine for. So, please don't use that word. *Muta* is better than *Libitina* and *Trivia* is not impossible. *"Please revert the rights of his book to his daughter, the author is dead."* Heart pounding. Hey slow down, it's okay, it's only a word. Papa's just sleeping, resting, maybe on a prolonged trek. Perhaps you don't even fully understand the word.

*Trivia: God of magic *Janus: God of doors and beginnings and endings *Apollo: God of sun, poetry, music and oracles *Muta: Goddess of silence *Libitinia: Goddess of death

Reclaim your space

Covid19 stigma: Do you not have a secret? Perhaps an illness? A situation? And you show bias and beat up those with Covid19? Or healthcare workers treating Covid19? Why the stigma? The anger? Beat, beat, spit, kick, kick, spit, just because you've been fortunate till now. Everyone on Earth who is human might soon carry a Covid19 *free certificate.* And you go about being judge and executioner? This is not HIV-AIDS, Ebola or MARS or SARS that somehow you escaped by some tiniest speck of luck. Most humans will have Covid19. Period. Full stop. So, suck it up, throw away your nastiness, anger and beat, kick, spit. Take a broom and sweep your mental and physical space.

Hold on, baby, we'll soon be home: Covid19's madness is all around us, churning, tossing, whipping and we bunker in the eye of the vortex in an artificial bubble of safety. We aren't home free yet, baby. At this moment Covid19 might be the giant in the beanstalk but humans are astute and like ants we build, and build, and build. It will take time but hold on, baby, we'll soon be home. Hold tight to hopes. Hold tight to strands of air you breathe. Hold on to any make believes. Hold on to dreams. Hold on to future time. Hold on, baby, hold on, we'll soon be home. We'll have our space back.

The crystal ball is, sick and tired, like Rosa Parks, like Fannie Lou Hammer, sick and tired: While beginning to de-crystalize, the crystal ball was sobbing and curling round and round, agitated. I tried to get close to reassure. It shied away almost petrified. The crystal ball doesn't want to be touched by a human anymore. It whispered to me, *"Why would I seek within to foretell future of those who are not normal in the present…you humans."* It walked away trying to collect its rapidly sickening, splintering crystals, creating its own new space.

The Ghost of Covid19: The murkiness of fake news. Fake people. Fake ideas. Fake injunctions. Fake promises, roaming the corridors of buildings now lying vacant. Covid19 stands like millions of ghosts vague about where to go. Race, religion, gender, plethora of biases still persist. Human race finds itself alone these days. The exciting, sexiness of finding alien beings, hearing their chatter on cosmic airwaves is receding like abandoned illusory space stations with no one left to watch over Earth. Gods of all religions seem jittery. Guards, receptionists, workers, timekeepers, bosses, custodial care, all equaled by a magnified rolling pin. Banshees are screaming in barren halls of working and living spaces and huge edifices are falling like baby dominos. *"We'll take virtual working,"* I whispered, stepping back, chest heaving. Will humans shed their fake spaces now?

Space generally: The West taught me a thing or two about regarding and guarding personal space. *Don't push me too much. Don't come closer. Don't intrude or invade my space.* Sometimes arms extended in front, a circular motion committed like *Lakshmana Rekha* to not come within or like *Ramayana's Sita* to not venture outside the pretend line guarded by *Vedic mantras*. Pretend, imagined or wanting to believe. Like unspoken treaties during cold war times. Myths, moral lessons, history tutor a lot. Can guide a lot. Can mold and control oneself a lot. But what about those who step upon, smear, enter, take away our spaces? Not during war. Not during enslavement. Not in refugee camps. Just during routine living when status quo is an ache and an itch. An eternal pluviophile, I walk in rain often, or stand under the rain showers in bathrooms. Like Charlie Chaplin, *"I always like walking in the rain, so no one can see me crying."* I busy myself dusting, washing, exercising. Or writing poetry. Or stepping and shimmying. Or being in my son's company. Turn off phone notifications. Turn off repeat intruders. Gently, without malice, despite all, reclaim my space.

*Lakshmana Rekha: In the Hindu epic, Ramayana, this was an imaginary line that Lakshmana drew within which Sita could remain safe *Sita, the heroine of the Hindu epic, Ramayana * Vedic mantras: Spiritual chanting from the Hindu religious texts, the Vedas*

My son's orange wedding procession

They say orange is the color of joy and optimism. Bouncing *kesari turbans* on most men, and women in wispy mustard, carrot, tangerine and emerging sun dyed saris, ethnic clothes or dresses cavorted in the wedding procession on a luminous, pumpkin squash summer afternoon. Most arms nimbly up in the air, fingers snapping with saffron, yellow and burgundy *maulis* on most wrists of Indian folks and bangles clinking on girls and women's wrists in the crisp amber sunshine. Folks were tapping and jumping to *bhangra* music as the air filled with flushed turmeric exuberance. Even the *dhol* players were wearing mango-colored jackets. A gold and salmon embroidered cloth lay on the horse's back on which the groom sat till the entrance of the hotel and then jumping off slid in to merriment with exultation and rapture. People staying at the hotel walked out curious and observing, clapping in gaiety. The garden of begonias, lilies, daisies and snapdragons also reflected a multitude of orange tints in the fountain pool. Vapors of gilded-leaf water glided by as I inhaled the fresh tomato splashed midday air and bowed my head in reverence to time that allowed a single immigrant mom to see this day. My sunset and bronze-marmalade jeweled chandelier earrings swinging like wind chimes nodded in appreciation.

*Bhangra: North Indian Punjabi folk music *Dhol: North Indian Punjabi drum
*Kesari: Name of a color that's like a mustard/orange color *Turbans: Type of headwear *Maulis: A sanctified thread tied at the wrist

They say people need to unite

Against what I ask in this modern world so ignited, so crass. Are we not one people, one species? It's kind of tiring following pundits and gurus spiraling like dominoes faster than Tour de France. And what could have been my child lay motionless on a beach. Who will hear her cries, his cries, your cries, my cries? Tears are cheap as they flow from eyes not banks. The stillness of the sand screams. The stillness... of the sand... screams. Please, shh... Can you hear, now? Why tell the heart to be strong when the mind has no heart, and the heart has a mind out of control? You push, prod, snatch, slay... lift her dress and sneak in, leaving her shocked soul rambling like roots un-synced from their pod. Did you listen to her body as you walked away vulgarized? Your core, sick of you? And then they were just chillin, arms stretched up, but you saw only their feet, tired and black. Your sense chokes, and you don't even apply Heimlich on yourself. Just look at your arms flaying. No censure. And then the first amendment is called to the stand freely allowing it to plead the fifth. Irony feels ashamed and my color is aghast, day and night it crumbles like fine wood left out to rot. Isn't equality the only color? Rest struggling for credentials, mock degrees in tow?

Claustrophobia

Didn't want to go back to India. Didn't want to go back to India. To the place where I was born but felt no allegiance. Its people, my people, gave me no refuge. In the last trip I sat huddled in one corner of the car back seat. Night lights flashed by awkwardly like pictures falling apart from old stale glue in forgotten photo albums. I was talking with my head, inside, repeating, just get us to the airport, fixated at every turn he took. He slowed the car, pulled over and my heart started thumping in dense mechanical boots like dark troopers in Star Wars. I panicked. He said, *"Let's make a quick stop for you to say bye to my mother." "We went to meet her the other day. Why again now? On the way to the airport. We might miss our flight."* Was he or his clan going to kill us finally? I was talking with my head again, inside again, kill me, kill me, leave my son alone. Or were they going to kidnap my son never to be found leaving me without sleep, dying awake each moment? Why did we agree to have him drop us to the airport? Like a horse sensing fear in an inexperienced rider, his voice become louder, threatening. My tears began amidst hiccups and I gasped for air inconsolable till my son raised his voice louder than his. *"You can't change the plan as you wish. We are going straight to the airport."* A grown son's determined non-violent Gandhian strength reigned in the ex. Didn't want to go back to India. Didn't want to go back to India. Not for a holiday. Not for weddings. Not for funerals. Not for births. Not when my parents were sick. Not now, not ever. But we did, each and every time, we did. Holding God within we went leaving my soul behind at the edge of *Arlington* waiting anxiously for our return. Even the thought of booking flights kicked claustrophobia into waking and gripping me tight, entrapping me in confined, constricted, narrow spaces. Like in a miner's shaft. Like in the space between the ground and the last floor where the elevator locks. Like in the sinking feeling of being homeless. Or being with an incurable disease. Suffocating, gasping and drained, claustrophobia refused to relent. Held on to my wrists, my words, my eyesight, my hearing, my footsteps. It stole my nerves, my youth, my sanity thoughts. At the airport he tried to hug, *"What did I say to make you fear me like that again? I have changed, truly."* You are emotional refugees, my friends back in our real home, America, said. I did not know there was such a label till we went back to India, each time, each trip.

*Arlington, VA

Flame and escape

I don't watch or read news after eighteen hundred hours. It feels more inhospitable, bleak, stark. During the day I find myself wading with those who died or lost someone to gun violence, murders, accidents, diseases, rapes. I writher, shiver, sometimes stare vacantly into nothingness trying to be them or their families. If it's taxing to bring myself back to kinder thoughts, what about those who were on the news? Why is humanity on a headstand even when blood clots pack tight the reasoning grids? If God had made our heart differently, suffering could be painted numb. We could have roamed in brain corridors still being innovative, yet our hearts could have been pumping like many *Datas*. Some would call that surviving, not living. Misguided or not, *Data* too wanted to be human. The other day, after turning off the television, after folding the morning newspaper, after dinner with family, I sat on the balcony overlooking the ocean vistas sipping Baileys on the rocks. Oh, the prim and proper, and luxury of the selected few. Not millionaires by any chance, though still very lucky. We are in the thick of winters yet the grazing of chilly winds on our lanai furniture upon which my body rests, cools my cinching heart. Young herring seagulls were flying towards the South while the older congregated nearer home. I too am aging yet primary colors are still perky and vivid on paper and in my brain synapses. I hurriedly lay flat the morning newspaper and splash my synaptic nerves upright and wholesome. I could decipher the words and sentences still blinking in the background like distraught ambulances, yet I keep my gaze fixated on the forest flame of my basic insignias with enough room between tree trunks for an escape.

Data: A character in the television series, Star Trek, The Next Generation

The above poem was inspired by the painting, The flame of the forest, by Indian poet, painter and photographer, Madhumita Sinha

My *Trojan* horse

Yes, we let our ego be center stage on occasions and my ego became the Trojan horse. I myself constructed the Gulliverian prop, then willingly revealed the path to the sanctity of my comprehensions. It proved treacherous and I made it clear to my conscience, I wanted to be found hastily. Many other horses joined my *Trojan* with necks twisted, eyes massive and bolting, legs twined and tails growing from navels, mouth's leering, hooves puffing, manes stiff like frightened quills fallen from a porcupine. A few men's faces focus on the fight, unnerved. Rest appears barren with cardboard cut outs filling the arena. As my *Trojan* horse fell on its back, the bulls came darting poised for the final denunciation. I upturned my hands to face the sky seeking alms of forgiveness. The bulls transformed into thousands of *Ganesha*, some airborne, some prancing, and one sitting near me engrossed, observing my expressions. I was able to walk away, ego bruised, subdued and ready to start anew. That night I pushed my *Trojan* horse into *Ganesha's* care to be melted and reused as asphalt binding me to modesty.

*Ganesha: Hindu God of prosperity and success

The above poem was inspired by the work of Canadian mixed media artist, Lorette C. Luzajic

Colors of the newly bought home

Morning creamy, canary sun held hands with yam afternoon tints, and a spread of salted butter, rouge and cobalt flowers near the doorstep said a perky hello as I'd come around the bend to check on repairs. My corn-peach palazzo with a string in saffron and tiger swayed like fresh mint green grass in a nimble daytime zephyr. Ecru, maize, squash yellow stones mingled with unwashed bricks on the outer veneer and inside newly painted vanilla walls fused seamlessly with citrine doors. The feeling of home was intrinsic like butterscotch on my tongue. Warm and exciting like a shot of golden tequila marinated with some hazelnut. Every time I unlocked the door, freshly squeezed lemon and lime drops walked gingerly in my path. I'd run to the third floor noticing every bit of colors on the way. The beams of light shadows on the floor, a track of rays on the walls, the stubborn heat on the kitchen porch. Opening the door to my bedroom filled me with a honey glow glistening on my cheeks like I'd applied sunset squirts. The young decorate the rest of the home, but my bedroom was my cheesecake and key lime pie. Tones of sugar, spice, clay, apricot, toast, copper, sienna, cider, tea, delicately sautéed potato colors flanked with chopped coriander and grape found their way in. Lamp shades were removed so I could see the oblong filament bulbs shine in their golden glory. Fairy lights hugged my bed and also tip toed on top of the cornsilk net canopy. With peeks of plum and jade bouncing on my *rajai,* the lights seemed like butterflies out playing eye spy. In the night they'd come alive like a caring personal galaxy of lapis lazuli. Let my body and mind rest. Serenity, faith, gratitude come over me as I slip into REM where fields of lavender tulips and gladiolus oceans have me chilling.

Rajai: Hindi word for a comforter

Native

Bury My Heart At Wounded Knee was playing on a jumbo screen on the expansive canvas of annexed fields. People were milling around filling the shadows of the agreeable and the pernicious. Each side in history believes its right. Arrows, bullets, tears mixed with the neigh of horses wounded in body and pride. Blood and the guilty swarmed like hungry, disturbed bees. And tarnished, tainted buggy lines had left permanent etchings in the muddied road in which puny-paltry minds pushed their bayonets into shoeless feet. And far away on the horizon, one could hear the wolves howling. And howling. And howling. A bison with lush green grass growing from its back sits at the entrance of a burning teepee village begging to be fed and eaten like before. The railroad keeps transporting. Even the artist refuses to let the train rest. The steam is chocking and scorching inside and outside. No onomatopoeia exists for the sounds of civilizational truths and lies.

The above poem was inspired by the work of Canadian mixed media artist, Lorette C. Luzajic

Fire couldn't stop laughing

She stood at the edge of a moaning and quizzing fire, with wing spans huge like wandering albatrosses flapping relentlessly. It's brows and eyes piercing and staring. It's body almost like hardened steel.

"What are you waiting for? Come on now, this is not the first, child, and it might not be the last. You know better."

"I will walk through you" I said. "I have no qualms, nor fears. But will I come out without feelings this time?"

Fire couldn't stop laughing. "Have you forgotten Sita?"

"Isn't this a different period, different story? I am choosing to be loved again."

"You think Sita didn't want the same?"

From the corner of my eyes, I saw *Sita* gesturing to be silent. I saw Draupadi signaling to do what I wished. I saw *Durga* and *Kali* poised to assist in fighting any new wretched monsters. Of course, Fire couldn't stop laughing.

*Sita: Wife of Ram in the Hindu epic Ramayana *Draupadi: Wife of the Pandavas in the epic Mahabharata *Kali: Goddess of the destroyer of evil

Sleepless nights

Storm: Sleepless nights are an aphrodisiac, sometimes. They are you and your naked skin next to mine. When hands linger, the morning sun is told to wait, and intense sun shafts are led out the room. In the middle of the night between endless sharing, sleepless nights are like that glass of water at my bedside in which I'd slipped a couple of ice cubes to cool the heat. Sleepless nights don't come very often, even though I send handwritten letters with a touch of perfume at the envelope's opening. I keep waiting for you. Keep waiting for you and the storm stands at the doorstep rustling dry leaves against restless windowpanes.

Lull: Sometimes, sleepless nights come like a lull between pregnant chapters of a novel. Curiosity compels me to turn the page and I drag my feet like exhausted stallions after a lengthy, tedious journey in medieval times. I try to reassure the pawns and the elephants that the mounts are being tended to, but one game of chess gives me away. I don my royal clothes and try to appear majestic as I stride out to allay fears of my ailing armies, but sleepless nights don't let go. Don't let go and hold on to the reigns like lonely seaweeds in a forgotten marsh. And the brittle leaves of the now overlooked storm have pressed dried as book marks in my prenatal novel.

Rejuvenation: Since I'm not the game type, I give up any lackluster attempts to try any more. Neither chess, nor dice, nor the war or love kind. I lay by myself for that's how I find peace to rejuvenate. On clean sheets after a lazy shower, I refuse to even put on my reading glasses or stretch my hand for the lamp switch. A nightcap of hot buttered rum and some Amazon rain sounds rocking with light Native flute soothes. Sleepless nights walk away. Walk away, gently, as I rest beneath a dreamcatcher with fairy lights blinking delicately. The storm and the lull have bonded, and the expectant novel goes to sleep, unread. And so, do I.

About the Author

Anita Nahal, Ph.D., CDP is a professor, poet, flash fictionist, and children's writer. She teaches at the University of the District of Columbia, Washington DC. Previously she's worked at Howard University, George Mason University, Binghamton University, Chicago School of Professional Psychology-DC Campus, The Smithsonian National Museum of African American History and Culture, and at Sri Venkateswara College, Kamala Nehru College and IGNOU, in India.

Besides academic publications, her creative books include two volumes of poetry, *Hey, Spilt milk is spilt, nothing else* (2018) and *Initiations* (1988); a collection of flash fictions, *Life on the go-Flash fictions from New Delhi to America* (2018); and four children's books: *Cashew, Vashew & Other Nursery Rhymes* (2020), *I love Mummy and other new nursery rhymes, When I Grow Up and other new nursery rhymes,* and *The Greedy Green Parrot and Other Stories* (1993–1995). Nahal is co-editor of two anthologies, *In All the Spaces—Diverse Voices In Global Women's Poetry* (2020) and *Earth Fire Water Wind* (2021). She is also the co-editor of another anthology, *Nursery Rhymes & Children's Poems From Around The World—You May Not Have Heard* (2021).

Her poems and stories can be found in national and international journals including, *Aberration Labyrinth, Better Than Starbucks, aaduna, River Poets Journal, Colere, Visual Verse, Spectrum, Organizational Aesthetics Journal, Setu, The Journal of Expressive Writing, Pen In Hand, The Dillydoun Review, The Ekphrastic Review, Life and Legends,* and a number of *Medium* publications in the US, *Confluence and FemAsia* in the UK, *Lapis Lazuli International Literary Journal, International Journal of Multicultural Literature, Mirror of Time, Writers-Editors-Critics,* and *Borderless* in Asia, and *The Burrow* and *Poetryspective* in Australia. Furthermore, her poems are housed at Stanford University's Digital Humanities initiative, "Life in Quarantine: Witnessing Global Pandemic."

Nahal is also a columnist and guest contributing editor for New York-based *aaduna* journal, and she co-hosted a monthly online creative series for several months in 2020, *Tan Doori Gup Shup*. Two books of hers are prescribed on university syllabus in a course on multiculturalism at the University of Utrecht, The Netherlands.

Her ongoing projects include a novel, a fourth collection of poetry, a fourth edited poetry anthology, and some children's books. Her writings focus on the intersection of race, gender, immigration, socio-economic status, environment, humanism, bias, injustice, and fairness. Nahal is the daughter of Indian novelist and professor Late Dr. Chaman Nahal, and her mother, Late Dr. Sudarshna Nahal, was an educationist, author, and principal of a K-12 school. Originally from New Delhi, India, Anita Nahal resides in the US. Her family includes her son Vikrant, daughter-in-law Sumona, and their golden doodle, Cashew.

For more on Anita: https://anitanahal.wixsite.com/anitanahal